Epistles/Now

Contemporary Restatements
of the
New Testament Letters

Epistles/Now

by
Leslie F. Brandt
with art by
Corita Kent

Publishing House
St. Louis

Other Books by Leslie F. Brandt:

GOOD LORD, WHERE ARE YOU?
GREAT GOD, HERE I AM
GOD IS HERE—LET'S CELEBRATE
CAN I FORGIVE GOD?
THE LORD REIGNS—LET US SERVE HIM
PSALMS/NOW
LIVING THROUGH LOVING
CONTEMPORARY INTROITS
PRAISE THE LORD
JESUS/NOW
WHY DID THIS HAPPEN TO ME?
PROPHETS/NOW

Paperback edition, 1986

Concordia Publishing House, St. Louis, Missouri
Copyright © 1974, 1976 Concordia Publishing House
Manufactured in the United States of America

Library of Congress Cataloging in Publication Data

Brandt, Leslie F
    Epistles/now.

      1. Bible. N.T. Epistles—Paraphrases, English.
I. Title.
BS2637.B69 1976   227' .05'2   75-38711
ISBN 0-570-03258-X

11 12 13 14 15 16 17 18 19   98 97 96 95 94 93 92

Epistles/Now

Contents

Romans 1

Do you realize that we have, every one of us,
    been selected and set apart for God and His purposes?
This is that Good News that was first promised
    and proclaimed through the prophets
    in the ancient Scriptures.
Now it has been fully revealed through the resurrected
    Christ, God's Son and our Lord and Master.
And it is through this Christ that we have been
    commissioned and empowered to communicate
    this Gospel, this Good News of God's saving love,
    to the human family throughout the world.

This is something to really celebrate!
The blessed Word of God has been enfleshed in us—
    and in our brothers and sisters about us.
And while we celebrate, we need as well
    to continually remind one another of this splendid
    task and encourage one another to be faithful
    to our appointment as God's children and servants.
Because of our great deliverance,
    we are obligated, indebted to every man, woman,
    and child in our hemisphere.
Our assignment is to love them into God's kingdom,
    to demonstrate in our lives and living,
    to proclaim in our speaking and writing,
    to reflect in our concern and caring our great God's
    love for each of His human creatures.

Yet, even while we seek to transmit God's eternal love,
    we are destined to proclaim His holy despair
    concerning those who refuse to embrace

His proffered grace,
who will not seek or accept the truth and who even
dare to suppress or stifle it in the lives of others.
They become gods unto themselves, these people,
and deliberately flirt with divine wrath when they
belligerently turn away from their Creator and
rebelliously move out of His orbit for their lives.
God loves and He will always love,
but never will He force or coerce His creatures
to accept His love.
If His creatures are determined to focus their lives
upon lesser things than God and His purposes,
God allows them the freedom to live with that
choice—even if it draws them into the inescapable
cesspools of self-serving and ultimate damnation;
and their freedom to exist apart from God becomes
the very tentacle that strangles and destroys them.

God grant to us the faith to claim His saving love—
and the courage to proclaim it—
knowing full well that there will be those who
will listen and live as well as those
who will doubt and die.

Romans 2

We recognize that some people, whose only concern
appears to be their own comfort and pleasure,
have no use for God whatsoever;

however, we had better be very careful about
    judging their attitudes and actions.
Some of the stones we are so quick to throw at others
    may shatter the thin glass of our own
    self-righteous abodes.
All sin is under the judgment of God.
This includes the faults and failings that saturate
    our lives as well as the wickedness of the ungodly.

There are upstanding, outstanding church people
    who are very narrow in their analyses of other
    people's characters while they are being quite
    generous and uncritical concerning themselves.
They, also, become a law unto themselves
    and are convinced that they are abiding by
    God's will for their lives.
They respect the doctrines of the church
    and faithfully adhere to its precepts.
They go through the motions of worship
    and participate in all the religious exercises.
They disdainfully snub or outrageously damn those
    who fail to accept or measure up to their precepts
    for right living.
And who is there among us that has not talked about
    God's peace even while we promoted the violence
    of war, or made professions of love while we ignored
    or oppressed those of other cultures or classes,
    or flaunted our apathy in the face of humanity's
    sufferings, our unconcern in the midst of
    hurting people?
Yet we dare to call ourselves God's children and the
    followers of Christ and seek to impress our peers
    with our devotion to the service of worship
    or the hour of prayer.

Worship and prayer, even the practices and exercises
    of formal religion, are of inestimable value—
    but only if we live within the precepts and
    prerequisites, the will and order of our loving God.
The authentic Christian is that one who is such
    from the inside out, whose righteous actions and
    loving attitudes are genuine reflections
    of a heart infilled with God's love and empowered
    by His Spirit and committed to His purposes.
He is the one who is accepted and blessed
    and used by God.

Romans 3

In view of the fact that church membership cannot
    guarantee salvation and doesn't apparently meet all
    the spiritual needs of every person,
    it is not surprising that the institution is
    regarded with suspicion; and some people insist
    that they can fulfill their Christian responsibilities
    and maintain their faith by other means.
Perhaps they can,
    but they are hardly qualified to put down the church.
Though our Lord made no effort to organize
    an institution, the net results of His ministry of
    redemption include the gathering together of the
    redeemed; and, in a society where strength lies
    in unity, this eventually resulted in what we know
    as the church.

Made up of human beings,
it is permeated with human error and disunity.
Nevertheless, it has been and continues to be the means
by which the Good News of God's saving love is
communicated to us, and through which we are enabled
to communicate it to the world about us.
And it certainly ought to be, and is meant to be,
a loving fellowship in which we can support and
assist one another in the glorious struggle of faith.

Church membership is of value.
It brings us into contact with the gifts of God's grace.
This does not, however, assure the receiving
of those gifts.
In fact, our faithful adherence to the church's rules
and regulations, rituals and traditions,
doctrines and dogmas,
may leave us no better off than those ungodly
people who have no use whatsoever for the church.
The point is, we are all sinful creatures in desperate
need of God's saving grace.

Every one of us must personally claim the forgiving
love of God by way of Christ's redeeming action
on our behalf.
Our good works and fine attitudes, our religious
practices, even our intense loyalty to the church,
are not sufficient for our salvation.
God's forgiving love,
revealed and made available through Jesus Christ,
is bestowed upon every one who believes—
who embraces that love—
and then responds to God's love in reflecting
and relating in loving actions

to fellow persons about him.
When we thus accept what Christ has done on our behalf,
we are then truly members of the church—
the true, invisible church; and we ought to be
willing participants and workers within our
organized religious community, the visible church.

Romans 4

It may be very subtle,
but most of us are still afflicted in some measure
with an insidious work-righteousness concept
in respect to our relationship with God.
Even in our proclamations of grace
we still come down heavy on the side of the Law,
the assumed dos and don'ts of the Christian life.
From the very beginning of God's dealings with
His chosen people,
even through such leaders as Abraham and David,
our great God made it quite clear that His
acceptance is not the result of good works
on the part of His creatures
but His own incomprehensible, incomparable love.

We are so apt to tie our faith on to certain acts
that we do, to rituals and ceremonies
and sacrifices that we engage in.
Whereas these activities are not without value,
they may nullify faith altogether and leave one
with the kind of righteousness that is unacceptable to God.

God's promises to Abraham and his descendants—
    we are the spiritual descendants of Abraham—
    were not to be given as a reward for those
    who measured up to laws and requisites.
If God's love is a reward rather than a gift,
    then what would be the purpose of or use for faith?
The law of God, summed up in the commandment
    to love God with our whole beings
    and our fellow beings as ourselves,
    is important to our existence here on earth.
This kind of love, however, is impossible
    unless we are clothed in God's righteousness,
    His saving love as revealed through
    the redemption of Jesus Christ and granted
    to all who accept this Christ as Savior and Lord.

We are to embrace that righteousness, that saving love,
    by faith, and then to act upon it,
    to recognize our obvious inability to measure up
    to the demands of the Law, to claim our freedom
    from sin's condemnation and eternal consequences
    and live as the true sons and daughters of God.
It was the faith of men like Abraham and David,
    their acceptance of God's order and purpose
    and their reliance upon His gracious promises,
    that assured them of God's infinite love.
We are even more fortunate because we have the
    resurrected Christ, God's beloved Son,
    who demonstrated God's great love for His
    human creatures and who became the means
    by which every one of us can experience that love
    and know that we belong to Him forever.

Romans 5

The truth of the matter is—
    and this in spite of those fine, religious people
    who attempt to placate God
    by means of laws and rules
    and traditions and customs—
    the truth of the matter is
    that we *have been* accepted by God
    through Jesus Christ.
This is where we now stand.
And this is what we ought to celebrate.
We can well afford to celebrate this
    even amid the difficult circumstances that plague us.
Whether it be physical pain or mental anguish,
    material loss or excruciating sorrow,
    this does not separate us from God,
    nor alter our relationship to Him.
It is when we accept and cling to what God has done
    for us through Christ,
    irrespective of our human feelings and frailties,
    that the very conflicts that beset us,
    and may even threaten to destroy us,
    become God's tools
    to grind and polish and temper our spirits
    and prepare us for loving and obedient service.
This is no vain hope;
    it's the Gospel truth.
God's love and Spirit *do* abide within us.

This is not something we have earned or merited.
We were estranged from God, the enemies of God,

from the very beginning.
And it was for God's enemies that Christ died.
It will always be a great mystery,
    something we can never quite comprehend,
    but it was this One, the Christ,
    who reconciled us to God.
What we cannot comprehend, we can still celebrate.
For it was through this sacrifice of our Lord,
    God's act of grace and gift of love,
    that we have been made
    the very sons and daughters of God.
We know that all men are sinners—
    that disease and death, physical and spiritual,
    have permeated the whole human race.
The laws of God,
    and the precepts of men
    who tried to find and follow God,
    were initiated to bring order into humanity's chaos.
And it was these ancient laws that revealed to man
    his inner sickness and eternal estrangement
    from his Creator.

God's love for man, however, is far greater
    than the evil that brings death and destruction.
God's grace is more powerful than man's wickedness.
It was this that was revealed through Jesus Christ,
    and it is this that grants us eternal life.

Romans 6

Regardless of our past,
    no matter how atrocious our wrongdoings,
    whether our sins be unconscious or even deliberate,
    our Lord's sacrifice is sufficient
    and God's forgiveness complete.
Whereas we shall always be sinners,
    and failures will plague us from time to time,
    the forgiven and reconciled children of God
    will dedicate themselves to obedience and good works.

We are now, even as sinners,
    the sons and daughters of righteousness.
We have, in effect, been crucified with Christ
    and raised with Him from the dead.
We are new people,
    focused upon new goals,
    compelled by new ambitions,
    committed to new objectives.

This means that we cease yielding to self-interest
    and self-concern,
    seeking our own gratification at the expense of others.
This is the way we lived in the past.
We have now been reborn.
All things have become new.
Having received the gift of God's love,
    we love and accept ourselves
    because God loves and accepts us,
    and we dedicate ourselves
    to loving our fellow persons as ourselves.

Whereas we were once slaves to self-concern,
we are now set free from its destructive bondage
to be the followers of Jesus Christ.
While we celebrate our redemption,
even while we fail at times
to reflect and communicate the loving grace of God,
this is the stand we take
and this is the goal we pursue.

We have discovered through sad experience
that there is nothing to be gained
through self-service.
It resolves only in disillusionment and aching emptiness.
The gift of God is life forever.
Service to God,
and to our fellow person for God's sake and by His grace,
fills life with joy and meaning and purpose.

Romans 7

Our primary allegiance is no longer to a rigid set
of dos and don'ts.
This is the way some people live;
they mouth and claim to adhere
to the Ten Commandments
or some vague system of morality
of their own making.
This is what they worship;
in such they find their security.

It is this, they feel,
that makes them acceptable to God.

Rules and laws are necessary
to any community or society.
They teach unregenerate men
how to live and work together.
They curb our selfishness and protect our investments.
And they keep us from destroying each other.
They even serve to reveal our human frailties
and make us aware of our self-centered aspirations.
They point up man's estrangement from his Creator,
how out of orbit and powerless his life really is.
But they can in no way restore a man to God.

Our allegiance is to God through Jesus Christ.
Our relationship to Him is based not on what
we have done for God,
but on what He has done on our behalf.
Christ has measured up to God's standards
and has taken upon Himself
the penalty for our imperfections.
We have been declared righteous, perfect in Christ,
apart from the laws
that are needed to govern our lives.
We still need laws to direct and protect
the lives and destinies of men,
but they are incapable
of turning sinners into saints.

The ancient laws do, indeed, portray
goodness and justice.
They portray as well
my utter inability to be truly good and just.
I simply do not have within my nature the capability

of reaching those great standards.
God knows that I have tried.
He knows, as well, how again and again I miserably fail.
I have the desire, even the will, to do what is right.
I do not, in myself, have the power.
And thus there is conflict, agonizing conflict,
    and I am driven to the wall in despair.
It is a conflict which, in one measure or another,
    will persist as long as I live upon this world.

The answer is in Jesus Christ.
God, through this Christ, adopted me as His son
    apart from the Law.
I am set free from the Law's demands,
    and free from its judgment,
        free to immerse myself in God's great love,
        and free to serve Him forever.

Romans 8

It's the truth; it's a fact!
We need only to claim it and celebrate it!
We are not to be judged under the Law,
    nor are we to be condemned in our Lawbreaking.
When we accept what God has done for us through Christ,
    we are delivered completely and forever
        from the guilt of sin.
It is just as if sin never happened.
This is what Christ did for us
    some two thousand years ago.

In the moment that we lay claim to God's great gift
of forgiving love,
it is applicable to us—here and now.
What laws and morals and rules and regulations
can never do,
God has done on our behalf.

And it is this that makes us
the very sons and daughters of God.
It is this, perpetuated by His Spirit within us,
that enables us to turn from self-service
and its resultant estrangement from God
to godly service and love of our fellow person
and to fulfillment and everlasting happiness as well.
It is this that makes life significant, meaningful,
and gives point and purpose to our living.
It is this
that puts us back into God's orbit for our lives
and welds us to Him
in a union that no one can dissolve.

Nothing, nothing at all,
can come between us and our loving God.
Our feelings of guilt and depression
will rise and haunt us,
but they will in no way alter
God's redeeming and accepting love.
Not, that is,
unless we live in accord with such foolish feelings
and neglect to hear and abide by God's Word.
The tragedies and conflicts of this life
will discourage us,
but they can in no way change God's attitudes
or stifle His love for us.

Failures and defeats may trip us up,
  but such do not affect our relationship to God.
Our boat will rock; the earth will tremble.
Revolutions will shake up governments and institutions.
Our traditions may be nullified;
  our convictions threatened.
Every temporal security may crumble.
But God's love and reconciling grace are forever,
  and He will never let us go.
If our allegiance is to God and our faith is fixed on Him,
  the very atrocities that seek to destroy us
  become the means
  by which He carries out His will
  in us and through us.

Nothing, absolutely nothing
  can separate us from the love of God
  as revealed and proclaimed and demonstrated
  through Jesus Christ.
We are the sons and daughters of God,
  His servants and disciples forever.

Romans 9

We are troubled about the countless multitudes
  of God's created children who will apparently never
  find their places in the family of God because they
  refuse or simply neglect to come to Him by way
  of God revealed in Christ.

What disturbs us even more are those masses of people who
have never had the opportunity to know their loving
God as revealed and demonstrated through Jesus Christ.
And then, what about those persons about us who appear
to be so good and loving, even more so than many of us
who claim Christ as our Savior, who believe they have
discovered and do experience God's accepting love
without reference to the Christ who revealed Him?

We know of only one means of salvation—
that which has been revealed to us
through Jesus Christ.
We believe, therefore,
that all who fail to receive God's love
as communicated through our Christ
are without excuse and will perish.
Does this place God in the position
of being unfair or unjust?
Our foolish reasoning is not capable of putting
God in any position.
God is God, and as such is divinely fair
and righteously just.
This makes it obvious that there are questions that
we will never be able to answer
and judgments that we are incompetent to pronounce.
God may have ways of reaching His creatures that we
have no knowledge of—and no need to know.
God is not inconsistent; He does not contradict Himself.
If it often appears to be so,
it is because the eyes He gave us
or the minds that comprehend this world are not meant
to peer into or fathom that world beyond our own.

God forbid that we presume to upstage or outguess Him.

Let us be aware, however, that we ourselves
    are without excuse.
At least for those of us who have been fortunate
    enough to meet the Christ,
    He is the way to God—and there is no other.

Romans 10

There is one thing of which we must be certain:
    there is no salvation in the so-called
    righteousness that comes out of any human effort.
Whatever man's zeal for good works
    or whatever his success in promoting justice
    or absolving poverty or promulgating peace
    or helping people to love one another,
    this does not make him righteous or acceptable to God.
We must submit to God's righteousness,
    and such has been our gift through Jesus Christ.
If we truly believe in Him—in what God has done
    for us as revealed by Jesus Christ—
    then we *are* saved.
And this is true irrespective of our race, color,
    ancestry, social status, or church denomination.

Let us understand, however, what it means to believe
    and to proclaim and promote such belief
    through our confessions of faith.
Once again, it is not accomplished totally
    through well-formed phrases or impressive liturgies.
This could be as phony as a sales-pitch.

Our pious exercises may well be a ridiculous facade
    that obscures the real condition of our hearts.
It may be far better at times to confess nothing
    with our lips but to let the love of God shine
    through us and by way of loving and sacrificial
    actions to reach out and touch others
    with divine healing.
To believe is more than calling on the name of the Lord.
We tend to do that every time we are plunged
    into some dire crisis.
To believe is to surrender, submit, abandon, renounce
    all that we are and have to His loving control.
It means that God and His purposes become the consuming
    passion of our lives, and His purposes point
    directly to a relationship of loving concern for,
    and action on behalf of, fellow persons about us.

To those who have not heard and do not know of God's
    redeeming love through Christ,
    there must be proclamation.
Yet, of what advantage are many words unless they are
    reinforced by deeds of genuine, God-inspired love?
Most of the people we meet have heard such words,
    but many have been unable to sense the love of God
    in the persons who have uttered them.
However, even if our confessions and proclamations
    are genuine reflections of God's love through us,
    there may be many along our path who will scorn
    the God that we proclaim;
    and we must bear the pain of seeing their
    continued rejection of God and Christ.

Romans 11

Of this we can be sure,
    even if His beloved creatures reject Him,
    God does not reject them.
It is true that divine love permits itself to be rejected
    and cannot be forced upon the objects of such love;
    yet it continues to love those objects.
It is possible that many of those who scorn
    our proclamations and loving deeds today
    may tomorrow open their hearts to the divine
    source of true love and may discover,
    partly as a consequence of our obedience,
    that salvation which comes through Jesus Christ.
Even while we may eventually give up on those who shun
    our attempts to introduce them to Christ,
    God never gives them up—at least not in this life—
    and we do not presume to know for certain what
    our God's actions toward them will be in the next.

We are often more anxious to damn the
    God-rejectors or Christ-scorners than is God Himself.
Perhaps we forget the patience and forbearance of God and
    His servants that was needed to bring us to Himself.
We obviously are not able to comprehend the vast depths
    of the kind of love that continues to pursue those
    runaway children until they are found
    and returned to the fold.
Is it possible that we are sometimes arrogant in our
    faith and even find a smattering of satisfaction
    in the condemnation of those who refuse to listen
    and submit to the Gospel that we proclaim?

This may well be one of our many flaws,
    but such is not true of our God.
How grateful we are that He persisted in His search
    for our souls!
How eagerly and diligently ought we to unite with Him in
    His persistent search for the lost and wandering,
    the willful and rebellious souls
    of men and women about us!
Let us willingly confess our difficulties in
    demonstrating our concern for the souls of our
    brothers and sisters and celebrate God's amazing
    and never-ending love for His human creatures
    wherever they may be found.

Romans 12

Celebration must be combined with service.
The relationship between man and God is a two-way street.
Our great God gives;
    we must respond to His gracious gifts.
Our response is the offering of our lives,
    the placing of ourselves at His disposal,
    for the accomplishment of His purposes
    in our world about us.
We are, once we acknowledge God's love
    and accept His salvation,
    under new management.
This is what worship is all about.
It is not confined

to loud singing or verbal exclamations.
It is turning our hearts, minds, and bodies
over to God's ownership,
and dedicating our abilities and gifts to His service.

We have all received such gifts for this very purpose.
They are not given to us to enhance our beauty
or assure our worldly security,
or even to make us more desirable or respected
among the people with whom we live and labor.
They are committed to us
in order to be committed back to God
in and through and by way of service
to our fellowmen for God's sake.
This is precisely the way in which our God meets
the needs of our neighbor—through us
and through these gifts entrusted to us.
Not all of us have those gifts that enable us
to administer or preach
or teach or finance important projects.
But we all have specific abilities—
love, energy, persistence, patience,
sincerity, concern, creativity.
We are to exercise these things upon one another
and on behalf of one another.
We are to care for each other
even as much as we care for ourselves.
We are to allow our God to reach and touch others,
even our very enemies,
with His care and concern for them through us.

Romans 13

We are God's children now.
We have been set free
    from the stern requirements of the Law,
    even the screaming demands
    of our self-centered natures,
    in order to live and celebrate and serve
    as God's sons and daughters.
But we are to live responsibly.
Even the secular authorities over us
    are to be God's instruments
    through which He governs and directs our lives.
When we disobey such,
    or fail to perform our obligations to such,
    we must suffer the penalty for our disobedience.

Nevertheless, our responsibility
    is first and foremost to God.
The authorities we choose to govern us
    must be expected to govern in accordance
    with His goals and objectives.
If their rule is unjust,
    we must seek to bring justice to all men.
If they seek to usurp God's will for our lives,
    we must obey God in scorn of consequences.
They may be God's instruments,
    but they can by no means
    take God's place in our lives
    and force us to carry out
    their wishes and objectives
    that run contrary to God's will and Word for us.

We must surely respect our governing authorities,
   but God forbid that we deify them
   or assume that they always speak for God
   in respect to our lives
   or the welfare of humanity about us.

We have been set free from the demands of the Law
   in order to relate to and be governed by a higher,
   more perfect law.
It is the law or the requirement of love.
We are to love God, and we are to love our fellow person—
   every fellow person—even as we love ourselves.
We are to love, and are enabled to love,
   because God first loved us
   and demonstrated that love through Jesus Christ.
Let us demonstrate love in our fractured world,
   and love as God would have us love.
Let us live for God and for others
   rather than for ourselves.

Romans 14

No matter how strong our convictions,
   or how ecstatic our feelings in respect to our faith,
   God forbid that we attempt to compress Him
   into set forms or shapes that we expect others
   to swallow and digest.
God is too big for our little boxes
   or our personal concoctions.
Whereas He is most certainly revealed through Christ,

He is not confined to the regulations and revelations
that we wrap around Him.
What may be good for us
in respect to the means and methods
of sustaining and demonstrating our faith
is not necessarily appropriate for others.

We simply are not capable of passing judgment
on the experience of another person.
His salvation must come through Jesus Christ.
The manner by which it comes,
or the manner in which a person expresses his faith,
is between him and his God.
Nor would we allow our relationship to God
to be determined or threatened
by another man's prerequisites.
Our love for one another ought to be generous enough
to embrace the other
regardless of the manner
in which we assume to comprehend
or endeavor to worship our God.
On the other hand,
while we must cease to pass judgment upon the
actions of our fellow persons,
we have no license to flaunt our freedom
in ways that may threaten their faith
or cause them to flounder.

While others cannot dictate
what I can or cannot do as a Christian,
Christian love will not permit me
to unnecessarily
hurt or offend them.
My freedom in Christ gives me the freedom

to respect another person's convictions
even if they don't make sense to me.
Few of us will agree on all interpretations of God
and His will for our lives.
We can and must agree on the prime requirement
of every Christian,
that we learn how to love and care for one another.

Romans 15 and 16

Without compromising our own basic convictions
let us work for peace and unity
in our daily relationships.
How ridiculous, how infantile it is
to allow these convictions
to build up walls between us!
Why is it so difficult to accept another as he is—
without insisting that he come our way
or meet our standards?
After all, none of us fully comprehends God,
even as He is revealed through Jesus Christ.
So much of our faith is intermixed
with how we *feel* about God
and His will for our lives,
and is affected by our personal idiosyncrasies,
by the circumstances and influences that blend
to make us what we are.
These differ with each one of us.

Our first concern ought not to be for ourselves,

but for our neighbor, his needs and concerns.
We are not to play God in his life,
  determining his goals and dictating his actions,
  but the role of comrade, friend, and brother,
  seeking together, ever learning from each other,
  what is God's best for us individually and mutually.
As we do this,
  we will discover that our areas of agreement
  are far more significant than are those things
  in which we cannot agree,
  and we will lovingly unite in celebrating God's love
  and in carrying out His purposes.

To state it most simply,
  we need to accept one another in the manner
  that Christ has accepted each of us.
If we did this,
  we would indeed find much to celebrate.
Our lives would light up with praise rather than darken
  our disjointed world with further disunity,
  and lost men about us might see something
  of the love and joy
  that their hearts are grappling for.

At the same time, we do need to be aware that
  there will be troublemakers amongst us who,
  though they claim the Christ name and insist
  they are living by His grace and guidance,
  are the very instigators of division and dissension.
We are to continue to love them—
  and prayerfully strive to draw them into the peace
  and joy of a right relationship with God.
Yet we must not be led astray by their pronouncements;
  we may even have to detour around them to avoid
  being entrapped by their distorted doctrines.

36

We are weak but He is strong, this great God of ours.
Let us stay close to Him as He is revealed through
    His Word to us, and let us spend our earthbound days
    praising Him as well as serving Him.

1 Corinthians 1

It is amazing to me how in our immaturity
    we tend to interpret God and to structure our faith
    according to the precepts and pronouncements
    of our human leaders.
There is no doubt that God does speak through such.
How else can He relate His wisdom and will
    to His creatures
    except by the accumulated experiences and insights
    of His many servants throughout the centuries?
Nevertheless, there is a fearful risk in placing
    all our eggs into one basket,
    in tying our nerve endings to one or two powerful
    or charismatic personalities that impress us
    as God's very special saints and servants.
If our understanding of the Christian faith has
    been pursued in this manner,
    it is probably very limited, even distorted,
    and we may end up with some human concoction
    about God and His will for our lives.

However men may interpret it,
    God reveals His love and redeeming power
    through Christ and His cross.

When self-appointed interpreters attempt to go beyond
    proclamation into some rational or human explanation,
    to subdue or dilute its offensiveness,
    to dissect its mystery,
    or even to add to it
    something that was never intended,
    they come out as confusers rather than articulators
    and confound rather than clarify the purposes of God.
The fact is clear: Christ died for our sins.
We are reconciled to our loving God through this Christ.
Nonsensical to some, offensive to others,
    it remains for us proof positive of our relationship
    to a living God,
    our perpetual and eternal acceptance as His
    sons and daughters.

Whereas God may use, even speak through,
    the very gifted personalities about us,
    the powerful, the influential,
    the very bright and talented people that pull down
    the spotlights upon themselves
    and occupy the great pulpits and stages of our world,
    history bears witness
    that God has more often revealed His purposes
    through men and women who were rejected,
    despised, imprisoned—even martyred—
    by the community in which they lived.

Whatever the world may think about us,
    God chose us, however weak or foolish
    or failure-fraught.
He has, through Christ, set us free from sin,
    even our subjective feelings about ourselves,
    to be His people—and to serve Him forever.

1 Corinthians 2

All of us are ministers of the Gospel.
We do insist, however, that some of us are especially
    called or gifted to be preachers and proclaimers
    of God's Word.
There are times when we become overwhelmed by our
    call or our gift and become more concerned about
    impressing people than we are about being the means
    by which God's Spirit communicates Himself through us.
There is then the danger of polluting God's simple
    message of eternal love.
We may be tempted to pacify or pamper our constituents
    in order to fortify our shaky egos with the plaudits
    and commendations of those who gather about us.
At other times we satiate our own guilt feelings
    with tirades upon the wrongdoings of others.
Whatever the reason, whenever we foolishly add to or
    take away from the utter simplicity of God's
    redeeming love, we obscure the blessed Gospel
    and may contribute to the destruction
    of the people to whom we preach.

This is a frightening possibility and should compel us
    to search our hearts and examine our feelings and
    our words to make sure that we are promulgating
    God's testimony and not some half-baked
    concepts of our own.
We are called to preach and bear witness to God as
    revealed through the crucified and resurrected
    Jesus Christ.
What God has revealed through Christ and through

His Spirit is wisdom of eternal value that far
supersedes the temporal and fallible philosophies
concocted by His creatures upon this world.

We can, indeed, learn much from one another
and from the gifts and insights that God gives to us
and our world about us;
but if they are insights or knowledge that contradict
or detract from God's revelations through His Son,
Jesus Christ, our Lord,
they are suspect and are under judgment.
Beware of those persons who insist that they know
God's mind on almost everything and who brazenly
formulate dogmas that claim to promote
divine will and wisdom.
Our great God has revealed through His Word and His
Spirit the knowledge and grace needed to keep the
faith and to promote God's purposes in the
world about us.

1 Corinthians 3 and 4

It is high time that we who are God's servants
leave our milk diet of subjective ecstasy
for the meat of basic discipleship.
We no longer have to play the numbers game.
Our great God does not judge our worth
by human standards.
Nor should we.
We do not have to always *feel* good

about our accomplishments.
Nor should we need the ego lift of popular acclaim
    or the plaudits of our peers.
We, each one of us, have a job to do,
    and we assume our responsibilities in accordance
    with the guidance, the gifts, and the opportunities
    that our God makes available to us.
As long as we are faithful to our task
    and in our witness,
    whether we lay foundations for others to build upon
    or build upon those that have already been laid,
    we are the workmen of God;
    and God alone knows the true value and effectiveness
    of our efforts.

The point is, our validity is not dependent
    upon visible successes.
It is granted and stated by God Himself.
After all,
    we are the vessels and vehicles of His Spirit,
    His visible hands and feet
    destined to perform His purposes.
The wisdom, the power, the ability
    to carry out His objectives
    all come from Him.
We are to take our orders from Him
    and give credit to whom credit is due.

Indeed, it is quite possible that our efforts
    to accomplish God's purposes
    will be condemned most severely by our fellow persons.
There are times when we may have to say and to do
    what we deeply feel He would have us say and do,
    and let the chips fall where they may.

And it is possible
    that, due to our human foibles and fallibilities,
    we may interpret incorrectly God's will
    and err in our endeavors to advance His kingdom.
Nevertheless, it is better
    to be subjected to the judgment
    of a loving, forgiving God
    than to submit to the condemnation
    of our equally fallible brothers and sisters.

How important it is to relate continually
    to the value judgments of our God!
If we seriously embrace the commission of Christ,
    we cannot begin to imagine to what heights or depths
    our discipleship will take us.
There will be moments on the mount.
There will be hours down in the valley—
    down where there is no honor or recognition,
    only loneliness and persecution,
    even suffering and imprisonment,
    as we seek to identify with the victims
    of war and poverty and oppression and injustice,
    and to communicate the love and healing of Christ
    to those who need it the most.
Whatever the rewards for faithful service
    in some future dispensation,
    we are the sons and daughters,
    disciples and servants of God.
Our appointment as such is reward enough.
God grant
    that we may be loving and faithful and obedient.

1 Corinthians 5 and 6

What is one man's hors d'oeuvre is often another man's dessert.
What is terribly immoral for some people is comfortably
    accepted and participated in by others.
What has been interpreted to be divine will and order
    centuries ago may be interpreted somewhat differently
    in the day in which we live.
Man's concepts of morality do change throughout the years,
    but the fact of immorality is always with us.
Anything that comes between us and our fellow persons
    may be immoral.
Any attempt to use, manipulate, or possess another
    human being is immoral.
Anytime we contribute to the deprivation or oppression
    of another person or cause him harm,
    or hold back from him something which may be of
    benefit to him, we are being immoral.

There is immorality amongst us.
It may not always be very obvious, or we may
    succeed in hiding it under our self-righteous
    condemnation of other people's weaknesses and faults;
    but in the measure that we neglect to love,
    to care about our fellow persons, we are immoral.
Of course we must stand firmly against those things
    which endanger our nation, community, society,
    family, and the rights of any person to be whole
    and happy; but we had better also recognize and
    overcome the immoralities in our own beings lest
    we be like blind people leading the blind.
How different it would be if we would all

truly love one another!
And yet it seems much easier to point up each other's
faults or capitalize on each other's errors.
The very manner in which we handle our own differences
and dissensions is often downright immoral.
Instead of accepting, forgiving, loving,
reasoning with, and understanding one another,
we sometimes blast off and strike out at each other
as if we were God's specially appointed saints who
are called out of the motley multitude to put this
planet back together again in accordance with
our opinionated concepts of world order.

We are brothers and sisters in the family of God.
God help us to act like it—and to overcome the
violence of disturbed people with love—
even if we lose our lives in the attempt.
After all, we are the habitation,
the vehicles and vessels,
of the indwelling and empowering Spirit of God;
and whereas we are expected to hate the sin
and wrongdoing that God hates, and this includes
everything that unnecessarily hurts another
human being, we are commanded to love even those
misguided souls who are unwittingly or decisively
involved in such doings.
We are also to love ourselves—
in the way that God loves us—
and to honor and respect ourselves enough to keep
our minds and bodies, our attitudes and actions
on that high level that will best enable God's Spirit
to use them for His blessed purposes and that will
bring health and happiness to our fellow persons.

1 Corinthians 7

Marriage can make or break, help or hurt a person
    in respect to his or her relationship to God.
Two people devoted to God and His purposes can inspire
    each other to be His faithful and obedient servants.
It is also possible for them to hinder one another
    in their faith,
        to make their own relationship so all-important
        that God has little place in their lives and affairs.
The marriage union is certainly no cure for immorality,
      but it may give proper expression to innate desires
      and passions that could otherwise drive
      a person to immoral acts.

Infidelity in marriage is generally defined as
    a sexual relationship outside of the marital union.
This immoral activity may well be the consequence
    of other serious infidelities—
      the attempt of one partner to possess or dominate
      the other or the holding back from one's partner
      those things that one can contribute to that person's
      physical or spiritual well-being.
In this respect, we have all at times been guilty
    of infidelity with our mates as well as
    with fellow persons about us.

Marriage is difficult enough for two Christians;
    it is unwise and risky to become intimately
    attached to someone who demonstrates no faith
    whatsoever in our God as we know Him through Christ.
The assumption that we can change our mate into
    what we want him or her to be

is a dangerous one at best.
If we marry, it had better be as God's children
and by His leading.
Then it can be a most enriching relationship.

As with all interpersonal relationships in the
Christian family, so marriage should be treated
as something sacred and permanent.
Divorce or separation is always a tragedy
even when we acknowledge God's forgiveness
for our errors and faults and for the failure
to make our relationship work.
If we marry for the purpose of giving to our mates
rather than simply draining from them that
which will satiate our needs,
if we always treat each other as total, important,
valid, and unique individuals,
and if we refuse to selfishly confine our love to our
small circle and reach out to love others about us,
the marriage relationship will prove to be
a satisfying and maturing experience.

Whether we marry or not,
we are the children of God; and our first allegiance
must be to Him and His will for our lives.
It is out of this kind of loyalty to God
that we discover our relationships to others
becoming truly meaningful and joyful.

1 Corinthians 8 and 9

I suppose that all of us tend to tuck God into the little
    boxes of our own personal experiences and notions.
Then when someone claims to find God outside of
    our castle in the sand,
    it frightens us and threatens to undermine our faith.
We sometimes react to this by hoisting our flags and
    shouting our slogans, hoping that we can drown
    out our adversary if we can't convert
    him to our way of thinking.

Sometimes I like to play the part of the adversary
    or the devil's advocate just to break boxes.
My purpose, or so I tell myself,
    is to set people free from half-truths and compel
    them to risk seeking *the* truth.
The consequence, unfortunately, may be that some of
    my weaker sisters and brothers, novices in the faith,
    may be sorely hurt and my relationship to them
    severely impaired.
On the other hand, it is my responsibility and joy
    to proclaim that glorious freedom that is an integral
    part of the Christian life.

We are free—to marry or not to marry,
    to eat and drink, laugh and cry, work and play;
    we are free from the dos and don'ts that become
    the religion of so many people.
We are no longer irrevocably bound to the Law.
Our salvation is a gift of God's grace and is not
    dependent upon conformity to the traditions of the
    past or the rules and restrictions set up by men,

whatever may be their claim to divine insight.
There is, nonetheless, a limit to our freedom.
It is revealed in that ancient absolute or principle
    spelled out by our God in the command to love Him
    with our whole beings and our fellow persons
    as ourselves.
This single limit to our freedom is imposed by our
    Lord's injunction to love one another.
It means that, insofar as such is possible,
    I must be all things to all men,
    that I become a servant of sorts to my neighbor.
Thus freedom becomes, for me,
    the enslavement of love to God and man,
    to preach the Gospel of God's saving love and
    to demonstrate it in my interpersonal relationships.

So it is that in our love for our fellow persons
    we are free and yet bound to tolerate their insights
    or lack of insight, their heartfelt convictions—
    even though they appear naive to us—
    without becoming bound by such insights and
    convictions; and together we seek to mature our faith
    and realize the freedom that is ours in Christ.
It is this, along with our own ever-present,
    self-centered desires, that puts struggle and
    conflict into the Christian life.
But it is all worthwhile;
    there is a reward for those who keep the faith.
It is not some sentimental, harp-playing,
    cloud-hopping nonsense.
It is eternal reality, the answer to our deepest needs
    and longings and the guaranteed result of faithful
    struggle in the Christian conflict.

1 Corinthians 10

A warning is in order.
It is possible to lose out on this Christian
    experience that is so precious to us.
It is true that we are justified by faith,
    but we are responsible if we lose the faith.
The failures in our lives, and there may be many,
    will be forgiven;
    but the failure to rise from defeat and
    to continue our walk with God
    may disqualify us for the final reward.
It is this that underlines the necessity to confront
    our conflicts with the grace made available
    to us through Christ.
We know what happened to many of our forebears
    to whom our God revealed Himself.
The same thing will happen to us if we ignore God's will
    and live by our own instincts and
    self-centered desires.

It is not right for us to continually discredit
    and disparage ourselves.
Our Lord is not happy with those people who persist in
    copping out by crawling under their inadequacies
    and inferiorities.
We are to recognize our gifts as God's children
    and see to it that they work for His kingdom.
At the same time we had better beware of becoming
    too presumptuous and assume that we are
    more special than others only to fall flat
    on our faces in shame and despair.

God does not relieve us of all of our
    struggles and conflicts.
He does promise, however, to be with us even in their
    midst and to grant us the grace to deal with them
    and to emerge from our times of crisis renewed
    and refurbished for love and effective servanthood.
Our individual and group relationships to God are the
    most valuable things we shall ever know in life.
Let us be most careful about them.
Our struggles will vary—our temptations may differ,
    but let us be sure that there is nothing between
    us and our God.

And let us do everything possible to excise
    or overcome those things that come between each other.
We need not be guided by another's scruples,
    but we can afford to be considerate of them.
Is it not truly Christlike to regard the well-being
    of our neighbor even above our own?
We need to strive together for higher goals
    in Christian living and relationships,
to recognize and claim our freedom in Christ and
    joyfully live and serve as God's sons and daughters.

1 Corinthians 11

Our customs and mores will change throughout the years;
    not so our need for love and unity as
    members of the body of Christ.
Factions and cliques are probably inevitable
    within any Christian group.

It may be one way of separating the wheat from the chaff.
But we need to be reminded that all of God's children
    are participants of the same Christ and become His
    visibly living, pulsating,
    serving body within this world.

This is no more in evidence than when we come together
    to receive the bread and the wine in remembrance
    of that supreme sacrifice our Lord made on our behal
He gave of His body for the purpose of creating
    another body, a body of men and women who would
    the recipients of His Spirit and the communicators
    of His saving love to a distorted world.
We are that body, and members of His body,
    with the unique responsibility of carrying out
    this tremendous task.
He assures us of His loving acceptance and gracious
    appointment and of His strength to accomplish
    His purposes as we gather often to partake of Him
    and to participate in His redeeming activity
    by way of the bread and the wine.

If we gather with malice in our hearts toward
    one another, we are unprepared and unworthy and
    may well be eating and drinking to our own judgment
If we come to receive from God but not to give of
    ourselves to God and to our fellow persons for
    God's sake, then we cannot receive at all;
    and our activity becomes a dangerous facade for
    our unbelief and disobedience.
If we come, knowing our weaknesses and shortcomings,
    to be touched by God's forgiving love and to reach
    out to others in love, then we come to be united
    and empowered for continued service in His kingdom

Let us come, often and together,
to celebrate our union with God and with one another
in the Supper of our Lord.

1 Corinthians 12

Pentecost was a great deal more than wind and fire,
or even the utterance of strange languages
by uneducated tongues.
The ascension or disappearance of Jesus did not signil
God's departure from this world.
It was to prepare the way for His entrance into
and His indwelling within
the hearts of every one of His children.
God, incarnate in Jesus Christ,
is now incarnate within a new body,
the body of His church,
His sons and daughters commissioned
to advance His kingdom through all the earth.
And with the gift of His Spirit
are those great spiritual gifts
that enable us to carry out God's purposes.

The gifts of the Spirit differ,
and so do the people who possess them.
The Spirit, however, is One and the same,
and this makes every one of God's children
of equal value and importance to God.
The more popular gifts are not the most significant,
even if they are sought out

and applauded by the multitudes.
Whether they are recognized as gifts
of preaching or healing
or writing or administrating,
or in more profound terms
of loving patience, enduring scholarship,
or courageous daring,
whether they be the gifts of intelligence or insight,
making money or making music,
they all come from God, these gifts, and His Spirit
remains the same Spirit in the heart of every man.

It is unfortunate that, according to worldly standards,
the one who articulates well or sings impressively
or performs skillfully on a musical instrument
or rates high in some sport
or captures the imagination and loyalty of the masses
through capable leadership
attracts the most attention and makes the headlines.
Other gifts, equally important but less visible,
are often little recognized or appreciated.
This ought not to be so
in respect to the gifts of the Spirit.
Nor do the more popular gifts indicate a greater measure
of spiritual power or of the Spirit's presence.
The church constitutes the body of Christ,
and the body, in order to function well,
demands the faithful and obedient response
of all its members.
God forbid that it be all mouth to speak or feet to run.
All parts must be honored and respected and allowed
to perform their various functions.
And God forbid that we set our hearts
on gifts of our own choosing.

There are more important gifts to reach for,
    and they are available to every one who will
    allow the Spirit total access to his body and being.
Above all is the grace to love one another,
    to share with one another, and to help one another
    in the way of our Lord and Savior, Jesus Christ.

1 Corinthians 13

The ability to be truly loving people
    is the greatest gift of all.
It is that gift which most of us appear to possess
    in such small measure.
We talk a good deal about it;
    we make grand statements concerning it.
But when the chips are down, we usually find our vaunted
    love in short supply.

We have little difficulty in loving those who love us
    or in showing some concern for those who will
    respond favorably to our investments in them.
If the time and place are right,
    we are even capable
    of risking our lives and possessions
    in behalf of a brother who is in trouble.
Whatever the reason—
    chivalry, honor, pride, or simple reflex action—
    our world harbors many heroes.
True lovers, however, are few and far between.

54

The true lovers are the people who are empowered
and motivated by the love of God.
Theirs is a selfless, truth-seeking, all-enduring love.
They love in the measure that they acknowledge
and experience God's love for them.
They discover that their response to divine love
must be demonstrated
in their relationship to humanity about them.
Most of the fantastic gifts that appeal to the masses
are temporal and terminal.
Love, authentic love, is eternal
and propagates and perpetuates love.
The ability to love is truly the supreme gift—
the gift to which we all should aspire.

I remember well the honeymoon stage
of my Christian experience,
those beautiful years when love was mostly vertical,
and I sincerely felt I was "in love" with God.
I am glad for those years
and for the thrill and ecstasy of countless hours
spent alone with God.
And yet I had little understanding of what it meant
to love, as Jesus loved,
the poor and the oppressed,
the refugees, the disenfranchised.
I was anxious that people might turn from darkness
to light, from sin to salvation.
But I was insensitive to the physical and mental hurts
that plagued a billion creatures in the same world
in which I lived.

Now that I am growing up,
I am slowly learning how to love

and that loving God is demonstrated
in loving my brothers and sisters about me,
that God has chosen to relate His love to this world
through me and others who have laid claim
and committed themselves to His love.
My ability to love is still short-circuited
by self-centeredness.
I know it is only as I rest in His love for me
that I will learn how to respond in love to others.

1 Corinthians 14

More than anything else in heaven or on earth,
I pray for the power to love my fellow person,
to break through the damning bigotry,
the crippling prejudice,
the stifling self-centeredness
that smothers God's Spirit within me,
and to channel and communicate divine love
to lonely, loveless people about me.
And I pray as well for the ability to translate
the message of God's eternal love into words
that will pierce the benumbed minds of busy men
and move their hearts to faith and obedience.

While others may revel in the language of ecstasy,
I covet the gift of speaking and writing
lucidly in the language of my fellow person.
Whereas a sign or symbol
of the Spirit's presence and power

may well take the form of strange, ecstatic sounds
and may even stimulate God's servants
to more radical obedience,
it is far better that we aspire to those gifts
that will more emphatically proclaim God's love
and reveal His concern for the human family.
The special, ecstatic experiences,
and the sounds that reveal those experiences,
may serve well to bathe dull lives in exquisite joy
and be of some value in one's private meditations,
but the gifts that enable God's servants
to advance His kingdom on earth
are the gifts of sacrificial love,
steadfast faith,
and courageous obedience that compels Christians
to live, even to die,
for the sake of Christ
and the salvation of their fellow persons.
What all of us who follow Christ
ought to covet most of all is the quality of love
that goes beyond verbal witness and proclamation
to the dedication of our energies and talents,
even our very lives,
to the bodily welfare and spiritual salvation
of humanity throughout the world.
If our love or concern for others falls short of this,
it falls short of our Lord's requirements
for an obedient and effective disciple.

It is necessary that we grow up in our thinking
about spiritual matters
and in our understanding about spiritual values.
The church needs the more mature gifts
if it is to reach men and women

with the message of God's love in Christ.
Those abilities, whatever their source,
   that do not benefit the church
   or enhance the body of Christ
   are of little value to the enterprise of God.
We need not deny the gifts or experiences of others—
   even if we do not understand them
   and may not even desire them for ourselves.
We must, however, concentrate upon those things
   that will give meaning and significance
   for our ministry to our fellow persons.

1 Corinthians 15 and 16

The high point, the constantly recurring theme,
   and the grand climax in the great symphony of the
   Gospel is the resurrection of our Lord, Jesus Christ.
He died for our sins and He arose from the dead
   victorious over sin and death.
If we subtract this from our message of love and hope,
   we really have nothing to say.
We must be sure of this—His resurrection—
   and we can be.
It was witnessed by many before us.
What is even more important,
   it has or can be experienced within us.

It is the resurrection of Jesus Christ
   that assures us of our own personal resurrection.
It begins even now when we are born again

through faith in Christ.
It is culminated in that life and experience that
    follows our exodus from this world.
Among the great freedoms that we celebrate
    is our freedom from the fear of death.
There need be no apprehension concerning that ultimate
    event in the life of a Christian.
Death is not the end but really the beginning.
It is not termination but promotion.
And this we know—because Jesus arose from the dead.

Maybe other people can discover motivation for
    good works apart from the commands and promises
    of the Christian faith,
        but for me it is the fact that death in this world
        is followed by everlasting life in the next
        that gives to me the courage to go on—
        and even to risk my life on behalf of others.
It is the resurrection of Jesus Christ from the dead
    that enables me to face death biologically and
    bluntly, not only on my own behalf but on behalf
    of my loved ones.
I sorely miss them, but never would I want to
    hold them back from the splendors and glories that
    God has prepared for them.

We shall, indeed, be raised from the dead.
Our God has not given to us the explanation of
    just how it shall be done.
Our three-dimensional insights would not be capable of
    comprehending it even if He had.
But this we know,
        the perishable shall become imperishable
        and the mortal will become immortal on that great day.
And this is all we need to know; it provides

all the motivation we need to labor committedly
and sacrificially in the purposes of our Lord.

Let us be awake and aware—always!
Even as we rest in what God has done on our behalf,
    let us be on the tiptoe of expectancy,
    working, serving, giving, loving,
    keeping the faith and demonstrating that faith
    to the world of men and women about us.
The time will come soon enough when we shall experience
    together the eternal wonders of the next dimension.
As for now, we need to hold on to one another in our
    love and dedicate ourselves in loving service
    to God and humanity.

2 Corinthians 1 and 2

The Christian life is not one huge bed of roses.
This is the way some have subjectively interpreted it,
    and life for them is the process of leaping from
    one mountaintop to another.
Christianity, to them, is always supposed to be sweet
    and ecstatic and running over with happy feelings.
It is also pretty phony—this kind of Christianity.
Of course there is joy and rest and comfort in our
    relationship to God through Jesus Christ.
We are to abide in the Vine,
    and good fruit is the consequence of such abiding.
However, let us make no mistake about it;
    there is also pain and struggle,
    suffering and conflict.

There are times of darkness and loneliness,
of doubt and despair.
These times do not change our relationship to our
loving God—unless they result in our turning away
from His eternal love—but they do sometimes lead
us through the gloomy alleys of depression and
discouragement and may sorely test our faith and
temporarily limit our effectiveness
as God's sons and daughters.
The paradoxical truth of the matter is that these
trials are very important to our faith—
and to our assignment and service in a suffering world.
As we participate in the joy of our Lord,
so we are to share in His sufferings;
and this means that we live and serve in these
valleys between the mountains, that we plunge into
the very afflictions and conflicts of our world,
identify with its human creatures in the midst
of all these distortions, that we feel their pain
and confusion and together with them struggle toward
the light and salvation that we know has come
through Jesus Christ.
We cannot just stand on some mountaintop calling down
our pious advice to the enslaved,
sin-ridden, trouble-fraught victims
entrapped in this world's gutters.
We are to go into the valley, the gutters,
the places where people hurt and rebel
against their hurts,
and there allow God's love to touch and heal them
by way of our God-inspired love for them.
We need to respond in this manner even toward
one another, sharing our joys,

helping to bear another's burdens,
supporting each other as disciples of Christ.
Yet we must not be confined to our comfortable
little circle.
We must reach out to the turbulent world about us—
to rescue the perishing and comfort the dying
and bring the light of God's salvation
to those in darkness.
As long as we are permitted to remain in this world,
it is for this magnificent purpose—
to be the channels of God's Spirit to a lost people.
This is what the Christian life is all about.

Praise God for the blessed privilege of being
His beloved servants!
Our assignments will not always meet with success
but will resolve in victory.
Christ is our Leader;
He has promised and provides for us His grace.
It is only by His strength that we can do
anything at all.
It is only because Christ has acted and has spoken on
our behalf that we have much to say and to do.
Now may God help us to say it—and to do it.

2 Corinthians 3

The saints of the Old Testament assumed that the scent
that ascended heavenward from the animal offerings
that fried on their altar fires

was sweet in the nostrils of God.
It may have been.
Sacrifices of another sort, however,
    are required from God's saints of this day.
It is the aroma of these sacrifices which permeates
    the world of this hour.
It brings joy and light and salvation to some people.
Others it offends and turns them into outright rebels
    who disavow God and perish in darkness.
We are called to be such saints and sacrifices.
The power to thus affect our world
    and to transform the lives of people about us
    does not come out of ourselves.
It is God's power and comes to us
    and to others through us
    by way of His ever-present Spirit within us.

This power, this divine scent,
    is released only by sacrifice,
    the offering of our very lives
    on the altar of humanity's need.
We are not assigned to demonstrate
    a new law or discipline.
Nor are we expected to pass out formulas
    for proper living.
We are here to proclaim and to demonstrate Jesus Christ,
    the forgiving love and eternal freedom that was
    released to all men through His great sacrifice.
This is the reason that we, the servants of God,
    the disciples of Christ,
    are the hope of our world today.
We can slice through the blindness
    of men's unbelieving hearts
    and reveal the glory of God's great gift of life

and set them free for celebration and service.
We cannot do this, however, by peddling the good news
    as newsboys peddle papers.
We are called upon to burn for our God,
    to offer our lives,
    to give of ourselves to our fellow person's needs,
    and to let God take care of the consequences.

Not all men we serve in this manner
    will respond in loving gratitude.
They may well crucify us as they crucified our Lord.
We have been set free from human ego-needs
    for that glory which comes through Christ,
    the freedom to live, or even to die,
    that God's purposes may be accomplished through us
    and His kingdom may grow around us.

2 Corinthians 4

We have been brainwashed into believing that
    success is measured by statistics.
It is no wonder that depression sets in
    when our successes cannot be counted on our fingers
    or even tabulated on computers.
The kind of service to which we are assigned,
    as well as the results of our faithful endeavors,
    are fully known and understood by God.
Even our errors are known, understood,
    accepted, and forgiven by God.
Discouragement will be our lot at times,

but we don't have to remain immobilized
by its tentacles.

We are vessels, clay pots, in the hands of God.
And every pot has its flaws.
God has chosen to deliver His eternal gifts
    to this world through such vessels.
He may have to break and remake us from time to time,
    but use us He will—with our permission.
He only requires that we gratefully submit
    our beings and bodies for His use
    and consecrate our efforts and energies
    for His purposes.

Of course we will have problems.
There will be times when we are flattened by despair.
There will probably be executioners about
    trying to nail us to some cross.
Our premature death is a distinct possibility,
    at least disgrace or imprisonment.
It is quite possible
    that we will lose our social status,
    home, job—perhaps even friends and family—
    if we dare to let God have His way with us.
Whatever we lose we will regain a thousandfold
    in this life or in the next.
This is the promise of our God.
And He doesn't shortchange anyone.

The truth is, we don't have to be discouraged.
We can be free even from fear of failure.
Only then are we free to live—or to die—
    to joyously spend and expend our lives
    for Jesus' sake.

2 Corinthians 5

The real basis for courage
    and the willingness to risk our lives
    as God's servants in this dispensation
    is our relationship to another
    and eternal dispensation.
In reality we have nothing to lose,
    for we have already gained everything as God's
    children and servants.
He has given us everlasting life.
Is it too much for Him to expect that we allow Him
    the use of our temporal minds and bodies
    in the few days or years we have before us?

They are precious,
    these few years we have upon this world.
They are all we can consciously comprehend.
But the same God
    who gave us this three-dimensional experience
    has promised us eternal dimensions
    beyond anything we can imagine or comprehend.
He asks only that we trust Him
    and demonstrate that trust in all-out commitment
    of all we are and have to Him
    and to our fellow person for His sake.
This is what faith is all about.
As a matter of fact,
    if we really knew what lay ahead of us
    in that eternal world that is to come,
    we would be too anxious to enter its portals
    and much too impatient about the few years

and many tasks and hard problems
of this temporal existence that crowd about us.

Anyway, we can stop being cowards
and begin taking risks for God.
We are the inheritors of His great kingdom,
heirs and joint heirs with Jesus Christ Himself.
Whatever we tenaciously hold on to in this life
eventually turns to ashes.
Whatever we painfully, responsibly,
and lovingly give away
really enhances our lives here;
and in the process of serving others
we serve our gracious God.
It is the risk we can well afford to take.

2 Corinthians 6

We are living in the day of our Lord,
the time of our salvation.
This is that day when for every man and woman
and child there is a way that leads to God.
And this is that day in which we ought to dedicate
ourselves to the task of removing every obstacle
that stands between a person and his God.
We had better begin with ourselves and be sure
that nothing comes between us and our God.
And then we had better see to it that we, ourselves,
are not obstacles or hindrances
to the salvation of fellow persons in our path.

Scores of saints before us have suffered all sorts
of things in order that their fellow persons might
be brought to God: hardships, poverty, imprisonment,
dishonor, persecution, and even death.
They submitted to one or more of these calamities
or misfortunes in the course of bringing Christ
to this world and in truly representing Him
upon this planet.
And yet these dear servants found joy in the midst
of their suffering, life in the midst of their dying,
great riches even in the midst of their poverty,
because they were the servants and disciples
of Jesus Christ.

Do we dare to be this devoted and intense about our
appointment as God's servants?
We don't have to posture as God's elected ones whom God
loves in some special way or has endowed with some
particular calling.
We do have to separate ourselves from anything or any
relationship that might compromise our commission
and make us ineffective as servants or
representatives of our Lord.
It's all or nothing at all in respect to our commitment
to God and His will for our lives.
God grant that we be faithful to our call.

2 Corinthians 7 and 8

It is not enough to boast, as some do,
that we have never harmed another person or

hurt him in any way.
The question may be whether or not we have helped
    to alleviate the hurt of another person.
Sometimes hurting comes before helping—
    like surgery before healing—
    but the end result of our activity ought to be
    the bodily welfare and spiritual enlightenment of the
    people with whom we deal.
There are times when we must promote grief, but only
    the kind that leads to repentance and redemption.
We must withhold neither the Law that drives a person
    to a forgiving God nor the grace that heals
    the wounds of His redeemed children.
And may God grant us the wisdom to know the difference.

It is as we think about the amazing grace of God as
    demonstrated in Jesus Christ, who enriched our lives
    through His willingness to embrace poverty, that
    we see something of the course He has set for us.
In the measure that God pours out His riches upon us,
    so we ought to channel them into areas of need about us.
We are not created to be reservoirs that accumulate
    but pipelines that direct the flow into
    poverty-stricken lives about us.
As we are the recipients of divine gifts through our
    Spirit-filled parents and peers,
    so we are to be the transmitters of such gifts
    to the human family with whom we have contact.
This is the way of God in our world today,
    and it is thus that He advances His kingdom
    through His children.
How privileged we are to be His stewards and trustees
    in the great task of making His love known
    and experienced on this planet!

There is a spiritual principle here with which we can
    well afford to experiment:
    the one who gives much receives much,
    and the one who holds fast to what he assumes
    is his has very little to give to others.
It is such a person who is truly poverty-stricken.
Let us love generously;
    we have nothing to lose save our own self-centered
    notions of what is of true value and worth.
We have everything to gain and the guarantee
    that we will be rich in terms of those things
    that really count in this life and the next.

2 Corinthians 9

Whereas we must support one another
    and help each other to grow in the faith,
    it isn't likely that we can determine one another's
    course in life or what God's will is
    for another person.
We can't play God in the lives of other people,
    though some of us have tried it from time to time.
We are to trust God and one another
    and believe that God will work out His will in us
    individually and mutually.
Of this we can be certain, however,
    that when one holds back from God
    and does not invest deeply in His purposes,
    his life will correspondingly be impoverished

and he will have little of real value
to give to others.
His own joy will then be short-circuited
and God's power through him curtailed.

On the other hand, those who give lovingly and freely
of themselves and their gifts to others
will discover that there is no end to God's riches.
There will be empty spaces now and then
when it appears that the springs have dried up.
God's grace, however, is eternally sufficient,
and He will fill up those places in our lives that
were drained dry by our giving to others.
And to our surprise we will discover that what
we receive from God in response to our giving
and sharing with our fellow persons is far greater
than that which we gave away.

We don't give in order to receive;
we give because we have already received
far more than we ever believed possible.
We have been made the very sons and daughters of God
If we really believe this,
we can do no less than give of ourselves to others
for Jesus' sake.
As we give we discover, to our amazement,
that we continue to be on the receiving end
of God's never-ending, ever-flowing grace.
Remember that when we give lovingly and sacrificially
of ourselves and our possessions to others,
we do, indeed, glorify God.

2 Corinthians 10 and 11

There are times when it is necessary to consider,
     amongst the scores of self-appointed preachers
     and prophets about us,
     who really speaks for God and who is merely padding
     his own ego or filling his own pockets.
Many of the sermons that saturate our airwaves
     or the books that make best-selling lists are,
     in spite of pious references to the Almighty,
     vain attempts at self-aggrandizement and
     do very little for the kingdom of God.
We must here, too, learn how to separate the wheat
     from the chaff, the truth from a myriad of half-truths,
     lest we be led astray by articulate speech
     or pulpit personality or the innumerable gimmicks
     designed to attract the bewildered masses.
There are obviously some very gifted people who cash in
     on their gifts for their own selfish purposes
     and who obscure the true and total Gospel of Christ
     in the process.
There are other popular proclaimers whose intent appears
     to be honorable but whose results are questionable.
And there are still others whom we are reluctant
     to approve simply because they are apparently doing
     much better than we are doing in advancing God's
     kingdom.

The genuine proclaimers and preachers are not
     necessarily those with the largest churches or
     radio audiences or the writers with the greatest
     number of readers.

Unfortunately, we are often more impressed by statistics
than we are by the quality of that which is foisted
on the public.
Whereas we must be careful in our judgment of
God's servants, we need keen minds and sharp wits
to determine who they are who are really serving the
Lord and to whom we may listen with confidence
and trust.
We may all be suspected and accused of having ulterior
motives in our pursuit of converts, but there
are some who are genuine while others are not.
We have no acid test that will immediately separate the
authentic from the less-than-authentic,
but we can ask certain questions that may resolve
in strengthening or destroying our confidence
in these people.
Do they proclaim the whole Gospel, that breaks
and then remakes people,
that disturbs as well as comforts,
that commissions as well as redeems,
and that resolves in thrusting the redeemed into a
hostile world to demonstrate as well as preach
the Gospel of love as revealed through Christ?
Do they present Christ as the way to God,
that One who shows us the Father,
or is our Lord represented as some superstar to be
idolized out of the context of His life and message as
related in the Scriptures?
Are they joyously proclaiming the grace of a loving God
that sets us free to love and serve our fellow persons;
or are they subtly promoting a closed-system morality
substituting tangible handles or standards, a
contemporary version of the Law, for that faith in God
through Christ which resolves in our salvation?

Are they just highlighting the joys and ecstasies
    of following Christ, to the exclusion of the risks
    and conflicts of the Christian life?
Is Christ, in their varied versions, a sort of policeman,
    magic-maker, miracle-worker, pressure-reliever,
    guardian and protector who shields His beloved
    from all ills and keeps them well and happy
    whatever happens in our world?
Are they preaching for converts to Christ or for
    contributors to their particular formats or programs?

Perhaps it's foolish to worry too much about what
    others are doing.
Yet, it is pathetic how many dear people are taken in
    by the questionable, half-a-gospel promotions that
    parade under the flag of Christian truth.
Of this we can be certain:
    the Gospel that we have served under is the
    true Gospel;
    the Christ we follow is the true Christ.
Our preaching is often faltering and inadequate,
    for we are but finite men and women attempting to
    articulate the infinite Good News of God's eternal love.
However, we are growing and maturing in the
    true faith and learning how to allow God's Spirit
    to speak amongst us and through us as we labor
    together in His purposes.

2 Corinthians 12

Some of our brothers and sisters in Christ
    exuberantly point to some exciting, cloud-nine ecstasy
    in their lives as proof of God's action upon them
    and within them.
Depending partially upon our emotional makeup,
    even those of us who do not necessarily insist on
    high feelings or out-of-this-world joy or peace
    as proof of our relationship to God
    do have those fleeting experiences of inexplicable
    happiness when it seems that someone or something
    outside of ourselves is dominating and directing
    our destinies.
Praise God for these cases of ecstasy that occasionally
    spice up our travels through the alleys and valleys
    of human suffering!
We cherish them—for ourselves and for others.

Nevertheless, our relationship to God is not dependent
    upon them, these mountaintop episodes in our lives,
    nor are they irrefutable proof of such a relationship.
Neither should we be dependent upon them.
We shouldn't waste our time searching for them.
They will come and go,
    but God's love for us goes on forever—
    irrespective of our feelings or lack of feelings
    about God and life.
God's Spirit indwells and empowers us regardless of
    the highs and lows of our day-by-day existence.

Over against the ecstatic high points of irrepressible

joy are those balloon-puncturing experiences that
    flatten us in despair.
It may well be that we need both in our lives to keep
    us close to our Creator and Redeemer.
The remarkable thing is that the Spirit of God is often
    more obvious and more capable of using us during
    these low points of our lives.

The thing that most often drives us into depression
    is some pernicious, unconquered fault
    or weakness in our makeup.
We are not expected to revel in our weaknesses;
    we need to overcome or control these inbred
    distortions that afflict us and may even harm others
    around us, but we need not crumble in defeat
    or falter in despair.
They may actually, though indirectly,
    be the means by which we recognize and learn
    to rely on God's promised grace.
God is great; He accepts us as we are.
He can work out His purposes through us—
    even in spite of us.
We need only to submit to Him our whole beings—
    strengths, weaknesses, and all—
    and let Him have His way with us.

2 Corinthians 13

We do not have to sit around and fret about our
    relationship to God.

We have become, through Jesus Christ,
    the inheritors of eternal life.
No one can take this away from us.
We are His forever.

Nevertheless, we do need to check up on ourselves
    from time to time.
Our salvation is not automatic;
    it is something that God
    gives and we must embrace.
This is what faith is all about:
    accepting what God has done for us through Christ
    and constantly living and serving by His grace
    and power irrespective of our moods and feelings.
Thus we do need to examine ourselves, to renew our faith,
    to rededicate our lives—again and again—
    lest we carelessly and foolishly allow something
    to come in between ourselves and our God
    and thereby stifle the power of His Spirit within us.
We need each other's help and support in this;
    and we need to love one another and learn how
    to work with one another as God's children and
    servants in our chaos-ridden world.

Galatians 1 and 2

I am constantly astonished and disturbed at how quickly
    some people are subverted from the Gospel as Jesus
    proclaimed it, to chase after some subjective ecstasy
    or go traipsing after a sign or miracle or vision
    or fall prey to some half-truth that promises

79

to make their lives more secure and exciting.
There are false prophets who twist the Scriptures,
   in or out of context, to say anything they want
   them to say, and people swallow that nonsense—
   much of it based on the ancient Scriptures that have
   not been reinterpreted in the light of God's
   revelations through Jesus Christ.
They enclose our great God within their own shallow
   concepts and pass this insipid and sometimes
   poisonous concoction on to their avid followers.
Their brand of proclamation may be popular with people
   but is not pleasing to God.
We need to avoid such promoters of religion like the
   plague and make certain that the gospel we submit
   to is the Gospel of Jesus Christ and not the
   pathetic mouthings of men.

We are all tempted, at times, to interpret the Gospel
   in ways that fit our assumed needs and do not
   challenge our small reasoning.
This usually resolves in some sort of compromise,
   and we are in danger of becoming content with
   something less than the whole Gospel of our Lord.
We need to shake each other up from time to time,
   to make sure that our reach for eternal truth
   far exceeds the grasp of our feeble understanding,
   to resist all attempts to bottle up our God in our
   small minds or to confine Him to a closed system
   of select rules, regulations, or rituals that we
   can handle without too much discomfort or pain.
He is the true God whom we accept and serve—
   and He is the One who accepts and loves and
   commissions us for service.
Thank God for Jesus Christ, who revealed Him to us,

and for His ever-present Spirit,
who works out His purposes in and through us!

Galatians 3

It is well to pause periodically and ask ourselves:
    is God's reconciling grace,
    His perfect righteousness, his saving love a gift;
    or does it come to us as a reward for faithful
    adherence to our particular brand of morality?
Let us remember that our morality,
    as faultless as it may appear to our peers,
    falls far short of God's standards.
We are grateful that our salvation is by faith
    and comes to us by our accepting,
    believing in, and responding to God's redeeming love
    as revealed through the life and sacrifice
    and resurrection of Jesus Christ.
If we are foolish enough to rely upon anything less
    than what Christ did on our behalf in order to
    reveal and make applicable God's saving grace,
    we are in big trouble.

We do, of course, need a morality, a standard for living.
We are not perfect lovers, no matter how devoted
    we are to God.
It is, nevertheless, a faulty morality at best—
    one that is limited to our human capabilities
    and which falls far short of divine standards
    even as they are revealed through the ancient Law.

Human beings cannot truly, selflessly, and sacrificially
    love their fellow creatures
    save by God's imputed grace.
We may manage some sort of respect for one another
    and even respond with love to those who love us.
We may feel a particular responsibility for people of
    our own race, class, nationality, or religious
    beliefs.
We may even go out of our way and probably risk our lives
    on behalf of human beings who are in dire danger.
And yet our relationships to the human family about us
    are so precarious that a structure of law and order
    is absolutely essential to our continued existence.
It is, at times, all that stands between us and the
    dog-eat-dog, live-and-let-live, do-your-own-thing,
    survival-of-the-fittest philosophy that has destroyed
    whole societies in the past and continually threatens
    our own.
Law and order, effectively administered,
    makes it possible for us to live together but is
    incapable of effecting a right relationship to God.

Only the acceptance of and faith in what God has
    already done for us in Christ will unite us
    to the divine Family.
Only that salvation which Jesus has made possible
    will make us the sons and daughters of God.
It is as the children of God that we embrace a morality
    that is far superior to the ancient and varied
    moralities and laws of man.
It is the morality of love—
    God's love for the whole human family—
    imparted to us and reflected through us to our
    fellow persons throughout the world in which we live.

Galatians   4

We who are Christians need no longer be concerned
    about identity crisis.
We are identified—and we have identity.
We are the sons and daughters of God.
To emphatically and eternally establish this fact,
    God, through His Spirit,
        entered our hearts and lives.
He redeemed us, adopted us, infilled and indwelt us.
We belong to Him; He is our Creator-Redeemer-Father.
This gives us infinite significance and worth.
And this gives us access to all the wealth and power
    of His eternal kingdom.

This was not always true about the human family,
    nor is it true even now about those who have
    not embraced the life and salvation of Jesus Christ.
Man, created by God for the purposes of God,
    chose the enslavement of the human will
    and its desires.
He is not able, by himself,
    to extricate himself from that enslavement.
Jesus Christ broke through the bars
    of man's imprisonment
    to bring him into the sunlight
    of God's love and grace.
He freed him from self-will and reconciled him
    to His heavenly Father once more.
Now we belong to the great family of God.

And yet it is still possible to lose that identity,
    to foolishly and tragically give way to the unruly,

self-centered desires of the flesh
or the plaudits and commendations
of this temporal world.
If one chooses to live by sight rather than by faith,
to value the security of this life
or entrust himself to its demands
and covet its rewards
rather than submit to the loving will of God,
he leaves his Father's home and family
to become a wanderer lost
in the wilderness of this existence.
So let us choose Christ, not once
but every day of our lives.
This is really living!

Galatians 5 and 6

We live under the law, the standards, the morality
that makes it possible for us to be a society
and to act and interact as a community of people.
At the same time, in respect to our relationship to God,
our salvation is not dependent upon the Law or
upon the rules and regulations inaugurated by men.
Having submitted to the redeeming love of God,
we have been set free from the Law's demands as
a means of salvation to embrace a higher law,
a higher morality, the morality of love,
which ought to guide and to issue forth from our
lives as a consequence of God's love and indwelling.

Whereas we are responsible for keeping man's laws
that do not come in between us and God's higher
law and purposes,
our eternal salvation does not come through such.
The same can be said for the religious rules and rituals
that are an integral part of many people's
approach to God.
They may be of value, but they can in no way
guarantee our salvation.
Our redemption, the gift of God's righteousness,
our total and eternal acceptance as God's beloved
children, is revealed through Christ and is to be
received by faith and to be acted upon accordingly.

Christ has set us free.
It is our difficulty in really believing this that tempts
us to put our confidence in certain exercises or
practices that provide some carnal or subjective
satisfaction in respect to our religious needs.
We even dare to assume that such practices may make
us more pleasing to God.
If we allow this to happen, we miss the whole point
of Christ's redeeming activity
and may even miss out on His salvation.
Christ has set us free.

It is in this freedom that we are enjoined to lovingly
relate to one another, to share with, to serve,
to support one another.
It is in this freedom from our need to gratify our
fleshly concerns that we can invest in the physical
and spiritual needs of others.
It is in this freedom that we can shed our anxieties,
our guilt feelings, even our concern about our
identities, and freely, joyfully, even haphazardly

give of ourselves in loving service to the
human family.

May we always be aware of those subtle temptations to
regress into periods of self-concern and self-service.
They are with us always,
these tendencies and temptations.
We know what happens when we court them and
ultimately yield to them.
Perhaps the best way of handling them is an even deeper
investment of our lives in the service of others,
a determination, by God's grace, to put the needs
of our fellow persons even before our own.

Ephesians 1

Truly, we have much to celebrate
as the sons and daughters of God.
We have, through Christ, become the recipients
of God's whole treasurehouse of spiritual gifts.
Even before we were born—
before the world itself was made—
we were destined to be His children.

Christ's death on the cross
set us free from the Law's demands.
All charges against us were blotted out.
Our sins were forgiven.
Reconciled to the divine family,
we are now an integral part of God's plan
to reconcile the whole world to Him.

It is, indeed, something we cannot comprehend,
   but God created us and chose us to be His people,
   and this was God's purpose and plan
   from the very beginning.
It was made known to us and made possible for us
   through Jesus Christ.
Through Christ and His indwelling Spirit,
   the brand of God's ownership was burned indelibly
   into our hearts.
With the gracious gift of His Spirit is the guarantee
   that all of God's gifts,
      though at present unseen and little understood,
      are already ours and will be revealed to us
      in God's own time.
The power that is available to us,
   that resides within us,
   is beyond our wildest imaginations.
Subjected, as we are,
   to all the weaknesses and liabilities
   of our humanity,
   it is almost impossible to believe
   that this God-given power
   is the same power that raised Jesus from the dead.
And so we grovel in our frailties and failures
   rather than stand tall in our faith,
   assuming that our small problems
   are too great for God.

May the Spirit of God break through the numbness
   of our small thinking
   and reveal to us something
   of who we are and what we have become
   through Christ.
He is Lord over all, and we are His church, His body,

the extension of this Christ in this world
to which we are assigned.
How immeasurably and infinitely blessed we are!

Ephesians 2

It is truly amazing, almost breathtaking,
and ought to send us into paroxysms of ecstasy
when we take time to meditate
on what God has done for us.
We were once the children of darkness,
destined for destruction, the victims
of our own self-centered passions and desires;
but God, through Christ, reached into our murky cells
to bring us into the light, to make us alive.
Indeed, He has done it for every one of His creatures.
This is the glory and greatness of His grace.

While every human being is the object and beneficiary
of this divine gift of eternal love,
only those who by faith lay hold
of this divine offering,
who accept and live by this saving grace,
can discover and experience the salvation
that God has prepared for all men.
Whereas God's love is a gift which cannot be merited
by human efforts to aspire to divine standards,
God's deliverance from sin and self-service
sets us free to give our lives to good works,
to love God and to communicate love
to humanity about us.

This is, in one sense,
    the real purpose for our salvation,
    that we might serve God and all people
    and thus fulfill that destiny
    for which we were created.

It is God's love as manifested in Christ
    that makes us equal, in God's eyes, with all persons.
And it makes all persons equal with us.
We differ in many ways—
    in intellect, talents, training and temperament,
    background and opportunity.
Under God, however, there is no distinction.
His all-encompassing love levels all barriers
    and accounts every human creature
    of equal value and worth.
There are no strangers or aliens in God's family,
    only brothers and sisters.
And all of us are members of the one body,
    the body of Christ,
    and are commissioned to work together
    in carrying out His purposes.

Ephesians 3

We are the brothers and sisters of Jesus Christ,
    coheirs with Christ of all the blessings and riches
    that our great God has stored up for His children.
As such, God has imparted to us insights to which
    our forefathers never had access.
It is these insights concerning God's saving grace that

we are to share with the human family about us.
How privileged we are,
    and how responsible that makes us,
    to live and love and serve according to the precepts
    of God and by means of the grace that He has
    granted to us through Jesus Christ!
As unworthy as we are,
    God has redeemed and declared us worthy to be
    the ministers of this grace,
    His saving love and sustaining power,
    to every human being with whom we come in contact.
This is our sole purpose for remaining on this planet,
    and it is this that gives meaning to our lives
    and enables us to discover joy even in the midst
    of the trials and conflicts that come our way.

This is a headspinning, breathtaking, heartsearching
    revelation that ought to drive us to our knees
    in eternal gratitude and free us forever from
    overconcern for our own sufferings and misfortunes
    and turn our whining and griping
    into perpetual explosions of praise.

May our great God give to us the ability to comprehend
    something of the magnitude, the glory, and splendor
    of His everlasting and ever-present love,
    and rid us forever of the foolish anxieties,
    the petty dissensions, the self-serving, legalistic
    concepts that come between us and our God
    and impair our relationships to one another.
Will we ever believe it?
    that God's power within us is capable of
    accomplishing far more than we can possibly dream
    or even dare to ask?

God help us to believe it—and to act upon it!
The crumbling, dissipating world about us is
    starving for His love and power;
        we are assigned to the task of bringing that love
        and power to the inhabitants of this world.
This is our divine commission;
    God grant that we be faithful to our calling.

Ephesians 4

If Christ is our Lord and Leader,
    we had better set our sights on His prerequisites
    and standards for our lives and strive to measure up.
For one thing,
    it means that we be kind and gentle
    and loving to one another.
After all, we are all members of the same body
    and are motivated and guided by the same Spirit.
This is, at least, the way it ought to be—
    unless some foreign spirit still possesses us
    and hinders God's Spirit
    from working out His purposes within us.
Why, then, is there so much bickering
    among the children of God?
Like jealous, covetous siblings
    we fight among ourselves,
        jostling, crowding each other,
        seeking position or honor above the other.

Our gifts, whatever they be, come from the hand of God.
They are not designed to give honor to one over another,
    but, together with all who make up Christ's body,
    to carry out His objectives and advance His kingdom
    throughout the world.
They are granted to us, not to make us more important—
    we already know our identity in Christ—
    but for the purpose
    of serving the human family about us.

It is time we stop acting like spoiled children,
    pouting, griping, criticizing,
    stepping on one another,
    insisting on our way or scrambling for some power
    or position that will boost our ego.
We ought to grow up, to be grateful for our status
    as God's ministers,
    whatever our parish or arena of service,
    and relate to one another in truth and love.
Only then, as the body of Christ,
    will we be truly effective
    in our community and world.

Do you realize how difficult it sometimes is
    to distinguish today's Christians
    from the secularists of our world—
    from the fun-seekers,
    money-grabbers,
    character-destroyers,
    warmongers that make up the crowd around us?
Is it any wonder that the world is so short of lovers,
    authentic lovers, redeemed and motivated by God,
    who will apply the healing love of God
    to the distortions of this world?

We may never be able to drown out all of our passions
     or rid ourselves of all our faults and weaknesses,
     but we must cease doing those things
     that hurt one another,
     that limit our effectiveness as Christian ministers,
     and learn how to be loving human beings.

Ephesians 5

Now we know that we are the children of God.
It follows, then, that we are responsible to Him,
     to emulate Him, follow Him,
     to soar within His orbit for our lives.
While we participate in what He has done for us,
     it is expected that we imitate Him as well.
As God, through Christ, demonstrated His love for us,
     so our lives, controlled by His love,
     are to demonstrate such love toward people about us.

It is this that ought to determine our daily conduct.
The way we act or speak, the company we keep,
     whatever we do—whether working or playing,
     resting or recreating, eating or sleeping—
     needs to be measured,
     not by what most pleases us,
     but in terms of what is pleasing to God
     and what is most beneficial to our fellow persons.

The fact is, we are under new management, new orders.
Our primary task is now

to reflect, administer, communicate
God's infinite love
to a distorted and disjointed world.
While self-surrender underlines our relationship to God,
self-disclosure should characterize our relationship
toward our fellow persons.
While we are responsible to God alone,
and are not to be enslaved
by the demands of man or state,
we are, by divine commission,
enjoined to live honestly, openly, and lovingly
within our human family.

As the servants of God,
we need not and must not dedicate ourselves
to self-gratification.
The Spirit of God indwells our hearts.
With God's infilling and indwelling there is joy
beyond anything and everything this world can offer.
We are to claim that joy—and live within it—
rejoicing and celebrating with one another,
giving thanks to God for anything
that may come our way,
knowing that all things,
even the painful and tragic happenings of our lives,
will ultimately carry out God's purposes
in and through us.

With God's help, and because of His great love for us,
let us learn how to invest in one another—
to lovingly and sacrificially give of ourselves
to each other.
This is the key to genuine and everlasting joy
whatever the circumstances that crowd in upon us.

Ephesians 6

Our first and foremost loyalty must be to God
    and His purposes.
His purposes do include our subordination to and respect
    for those who are over and above us,
    children to parents, students to teachers,
    employees to employers.
It is, however, within God's purposes that those who
    hold such superior positions do so by God's direction,
    and they are responsible for wise and loving
    leadership.
Nevertheless, in our allegiance to God we are to
    courageously resist anyone, whether it be individual
    or government, who tries to play god over our lives
    and who attempts to coerce us into actions
    that are opposed to God's will and plan for us.

The Christian walk is never easy.
There are enemies to contend with,
    obstacles to confront, and they must be opposed
    and overcome in the power and Spirit of God.
Whether these enemies,
    these spiritual forces of darkness,
    work through the power structures over us or the
    numerous loopholes that plague our individual lives,
    we must learn how to recognize who and what
    they are and resist them whenever they appear.

If we are to be strong and courageous in the face
    of enemy forces far stronger than we are,
    we must lean on that power that is made available

to us through Jesus Christ.
For one thing,
    we must be intense in our search for truth.
Christ has revealed to us all that we need to know
    in order to experience God's saving love.
Yet we must always be open to ever deeper revelations
    and experiences of divine love while being very wary
    of anyone who detracts from or adds to that which
    has been revealed through Christ.
And then we must beware of those who subtly or
    erroneously attempt to pull us back into the bondage
    of salvation-by-works and thus enslave us in some
    man-made system of morality that portends to please
    God.
We are clothed in God's righteousness,
    gifted with His salvation.
Nothing can change that—save our neglect
    to act upon it.
We must walk in God's path for our lives,
    the path of loving service to our fellow persons
    for His sake.
When we fill our minds and commit our lives
    to His Word and His will for us,
    our bodies will respond accordingly.
We must continually shun the tentacles of the Law
    that seek to draw us back into its stifling embrace
    and walk and run, work and serve with our faith
    centered upon that One who made us His own through
    Jesus Christ.
We must keep awake and be aware—
    and joyously and freely abandon ourselves
    to loving God and allowing Him to communicate His love
    through our love for our fellow persons.

Philippians 1

I have met some beautiful people
    in the course of my travels.
They are my sisters and brothers in Christ,
    fellow servants in the kingdom-work of God.
Every time I think about them, I do so prayerfully,
    and a surge of joy fills my heart.
God spoke to me, comforted me in my despair,
    and through these people challenged me in my apathy.
I pray that God will continue to use them
    to reach others
    even as He used them to undergird and uplift me
    and that what He has begun in us He will continue
    until we are brought together
    in everlasting fellowship
    in that dimension beyond this life and world.

It is truly amazing to me,
    and it should be encouraging to all of us,
    the way in which God is able
    to turn the unhappy things
    that happen to us,
    even our foolish errors and failures,
    into steppingstones toward the accomplishment
    of His purposes in our world.
Even the apparent ego trips
    of certain Christian evangelists,
    who preach more for crowds than they do for Christ,
    are sometimes utilized to promote the Gospel and
    advance the cause of the Kingdom.
We have so much to celebrate.

God has not given up on our world.
He is here and sometimes because of us,
    sometimes in spite of us,
    He is working out His purposes in our world.

Our greatest concern at this point is
    that we do not fail
    to give God our all, and to risk our all,
    that His purposes might be accomplished through us.
It means that we be willing
    to put our lives on the line,
    to live and, if need be, to die,
    to fulfill our commission
    as God's soldiers and servants.
We have nothing to lose and we have nothing
    to be afraid of.
It is not surprising that we cling
    so tenaciously to this life.
It is all that our natural senses can comprehend.
Nevertheless, if we knew what God has in store for us,
    we would have no fear whatsoever of death
    and whatever may follow death.
We would probably be most eager
    to leave this vale of tears
    for the indescribable glories of life eternal.
We are here in the valley under divine orders.
Let us be alive and courageous and joyful and obedient
    as we faithfully carry out God's commission to us.

Philippians 2

There is a way to test the authenticity
  of our relationship with God;
  it is by examining our relationships
  to our fellow persons.
When we are short on compassion and concern
  for our brothers and sisters,
  it is probably because we haven't fully grasped
  or experienced God's infinite love for us.
God is not holding back; His love is available.
And so is His great wealth and power and all
  the other gifts needed to enrich our lives
  and make us happy and secure.
They are, however, gifts
  that must be shared with others
  lest they turn to ashes in our hands.

There are, unfortunately, ambitious Christians
  who are more concerned
  about their own image
  than the needs of their fellow person.
They attempt to corral their God-given gifts
  for their own egocentric purposes.
This was not so with Jesus Christ.
Even though He was filled with the power of God,
  He never used it for His own glory or gratification.
He became a servant of men,
  using His divine power only to heal their hurts
  and free their spirits and reveal to them
  their rich inheritance as the children of God.
As God incarnate, Christ walked as man upon this earth—

even through the experiences of torture and death—
that He might touch human creatures
with the love of their Father in heaven.
Now we are assigned to be Christs incarnate—
proclaiming, demonstrating, and communicating
God's healing, reconciling love to one another
and to His wandering,
lonely, lost children around us.

We have wept and whined long enough.
It is time we claim God's proffered gifts
and begin to act responsively
as His divinely endowed servants.
Whereas we, as fallible human beings,
may claim the right to be imperfect,
we have, as well, the responsibility to focus
upon God's goals for our lives
and to become more and more
like the Christ who brought us to our God.
Now, as God's redeemed and restored children,
we are commissioned and assigned to brighten up
this dark world like stars that light up the night.
And like those stars that reflect the sun's glory
after darkness has fallen,
we are to spell out the promise of the coming dawn.
Our objective is the redemption of all men,
that every creature of God might honor the God
of his creation and be restored to His orbit
and destiny for his life.

Philippians 3

I suppose we must always be on our guard
    against those sectarians and cultists
    who wrap their lives
    about their own private experiences and rituals
    and then damn us
    for not buying into their product.
We ought to be mature enough to avoid such entrapments.
We need to love these people,
    but we don't have to follow them.
We are aware of the inability of ceremonies
    to make us or keep us Christian.
We need Jesus Christ and His righteousness.
It is He whom we follow; He is the One whom we serve.
So much of what goes on in the name of religion
    is plain garbage and should be treated as such.
We can afford to respect another man's opinions—
    we are hardly capable of denying his experiences—
    but if he adds to or subtracts from what God
    through Christ has done for us,
    then his gospel is not for us
    and we ought to avoid it like the plague.

Jesus Christ is sufficient—
    and so is the righteousness that He imparts to us.
We don't earn or merit or gain it by following
    certain rules or rituals;
    we receive it as the gift of God's love.
We possess this righteousness
    even now by faith in Christ.
We have no need for any other.

This by no means indicates that we have arrived—
    that we have already reached the ultimate
    in our natural state of being.
We do, indeed, belong to God; we are His possession.
And yet we struggle constantly
    to surrender our total beings to Him
    —to let Him have His way with us.
This does not come easily.
It involves the crucible of conflict—
    even failure and defeat.
But even when we fall, we fall only to rise again.
Acknowledging but never nursing our failures,
    we claim God's gracious forgiveness and carry on,
    knowing that our loving God understands
    and perpetually reaches out to draw us to Himself.
Even while we are God's sons and daughters,
    we are in the process of *becoming*.
Our creation is not yet completed
    and won't be until we break through this mortal shell
    to become perfectly and eternally united to God.
Meanwhile our citizenship is in God's kingdom,
    and we are here to advance that kingdom
    throughout our sorry world.

Philippians 4

It is my fondest wish that God's children be happy.
I don't mean ecstatic or continually exuberant;
    I mean happy, full of joy,

that deep-down contentment that persists
even in the midst of trials and tribulations
and difficult circumstances.
As the very children of God,
we really don't have a thing to worry about.
Whatever our real needs,
we know that God will fulfill them in His own time
and in accordance with His will.
We can well afford to celebrate,
to live in thankfulness,
and to allow the incomprehensible peace of God
to mend the frayed edges of our troubled lives
and make us serene and secure in our Christian faith.

It is not easy, but worthy of every effort,
to cast out the troublesome demons that plague us
and to think and to act positively.
The unfortunate happenings that beset us
should not cheat us out of the joy
that comes through Christ.
We don't have to allow these things
to come between us and our God.

Whether we are rich or poor,
in the valley or on the mount,
whether there be sorrow or pain
or conflict or defeat,
this need not threaten our relationship with God.
We belong to Him,
and if we think and act as if we belong to Him,
nothing will alter that glorious relationship.
We are His forever, and we can celebrate forever
our adoption and our identity
as His sons and daughters.

And He will provide us
  with the strength and the courage
  that we need to confront and overcome
  anything that comes our way.

Colossians 1

How grateful we are to God for what He has done for us,
  for the clear revelation of His love through His Son,
  our Savior and Lord, Jesus Christ!
It is through this Christ that we have experienced
  redemption and forgiveness.
It is by way of Christ that we have been set free
  from the bondage of darkness and despair.
It is in Christ that we become the very heirs of God
  and share in the inheritance promised to all of
  His sons and daughters from the beginning of time.
He is full of God, this Jesus, God incarnate,
  the Word become flesh,
  and manifests all of the glory and beauty,
  the splendor and majesty, the love and grace that
  is possible for the human mind and heart to comprehend.
We can only know God as He is revealed through this
  Christ; and so Christ then becomes for us that One who
  puts it all together, the head of the body and of the
  church, our Lord and Leader, our Shepherd and King.

We, who were once living unto ourselves, focusing our
  allegiance upon people or things that served our
  self-interests, and were attempting to pacify or

cover over our inner feelings of guilt by way of
occasional good works or religious exercises,
have now been brought into the family of God
through the life, death, and resurrection of
Jesus Christ; and we have through Christ been
accepted by God as holy, righteous, and without blame.
We cannot possibly comprehend it,
but we can accept it as an accomplished fact.
We are the sons and daughters of God
and are as close to Him and loved by Him
as is His Son, Jesus Christ.
It is now our responsibility not only to have faith,
but to keep the faith.
It is our commission, as God's children,
to allow the God incarnate in Christ
to become incarnate in us and through us,
to reveal, through word and deed,
His saving love to fellow persons about us.
May God through His indwelling Spirit enable us to
mature, to grow up, and to become fruitful
and effective channels of His redeeming love and
healing power to the world in which we live.

Colossians 2

To be mature as Christians means that we continually
grow in the faith that we have embraced.
It is not sufficient to verbally and emotionally
receive Christ.

We are to be perpetually open to God as He is
    fully revealed in Christ and as He continues
    to instruct and establish us through His Spirit.
As we cannot know God save through Christ,
    so we cannot hear God speak or carry out our
    allegiance to God unless we listen to Christ's words
    and follow His leading in our daily lives and
    activities.
If there is anyone who claims to have found God
    apart from Christ or who insists that he can
    determine and follow God's will apart from our Lord's
    revelations and proclamations,
    he is a usurper, a false prophet,
    and ought to be resisted or avoided.

There are many legalists about who attempt to cramp
    God into some ethical formula that they pass
    out as a requisite for God's acceptance and salvation.
Their man-made religions are popular with multitudes
    of people because they provide handles or rungs in a
    ladder by which human beings can ultimately
    approach and please the Deity.
They are preaching Law, not grace,
    or mostly Law with a smattering of grace.
As attractive as may be their declarations
    and devoted their religious activities and promotions,
    they are proclaiming a false gospel;
    and it would be better that we not listen to them
    lest we be naively sucked into their immature,
    if not outright devious, babblings.

Colossians 3 and 4

I wonder if we really understand it,
    that we are the people of God,
    that He loves us and chooses that we be His people.
Now we are really alive!
As Christ was raised from the dead,
    so we have been brought from death to life
    and shall live forever.
We must set our hearts and fix our minds
    on this fantastic truth.
Faith means that we begin to live and act as if
    this is the truth, that this really happened,
    whether we feel it or not.

There are, however, still some things within us
    which must not be permitted
    to control our thinking or activities.
They are those things that come between us and God
    and are capable of causing harm to our fellow person.
Still rising out of the darkness to haunt and tempt us
    are the shadows of greed and lust
    and hostility and deceit,
    booby traps that can destroy us
    and anyone close to us.
We must, by God's grace and His power at work within us,
    blast these insidious demons out of our lives.
And we must do so again and again,
    for they die hard, these agents of death.

Thus we must grow in the faith,
    allowing the Spirit of God

to captivate and subordinate
every aspect of our being under His purging love.
We must plug up these loopholes in our lives
by focusing continually upon God and His love
and permit Him to flood our hearts with His love.
And we must determinedly and actively exercise that
inflowing and outgoing love by reaching out
to others in concern and compassion.

We are to begin doing this
with those who are near us.
We must start right where we are—
even with our comrades in Christ—
by being open, honest, truthful, nonjudgmental,
manifesting patience and understanding,
forgiving them as God indeed forgives us,
allowing God's love to spill over our lives
into the troubled lives of others.
But God forbid that our love be limited
to our own kind.
It is God's love that reaches out to others
through our love,
and God's love is destined for all mankind,
the whole human family, slave and free,
rich and poor, black and white.
What we do in our interpersonal relationships
we are to do
as the children of God,
the disciples of Jesus Christ,
in the spirit of celebration and thanksgiving.
Let us give ourselves over to prayer and thanksgiving
and conduct ourselves like the children and
servants of God,
acknowledging that the hours of our days and the

words of our mouths are under contract
to our Savior and Lord.
And may God so guide us and control us that we always
speak and act in accordance with His will for our
lives.

1 Thessalonians 1 and 2

We are thankful for the family of God,
the followers of Christ who are faithfully
laboring within His purposes.
Some of them are on the front lines in positions of
great risk to health and life.
Others are quietly and profoundly pursuing God's
objectives in places and in ways that are unknown
to us.
We applaud our brothers and sisters and pray that God
will grant them much joy and fill them with His
power as they strive to advance His kingdom.
Their devotion to our Lord,
their dedication to the needs of people,
ought to shame us in our lethargy and encourage us
in our times of depression and urge us on toward
a more radical obedience to our Lord and Master.

It is obviously not our primary concern to be popular
with the people with whom we deal even though we are
charged with the task of loving and serving them.
We are, first and foremost, to please God, to serve Him,

and this may not earn for us the commendations
of the crowd.
It will, if we are faithful,
result in our Lord's commendations.
It is important, however, that we commend one another,
that we encourage and support our colaborers
in whatever ways we can.
The task is difficult; the road is rough for all of us.
We need, from time to time, the feeling of strong,
loving, undergirding arms to enable us to bear
the burdens of our respective ministries.
Indeed, the joy and strength that comes to us
in our labors will often come
in our love and concern for one another.

Along with our prayers on each other's behalf,
let us write and speak and reach out through
loving embraces to transmit messages of joy and love
to our brothers and sisters about us.
There are those within the Christian family who are
enmeshed within deep conflicts and who are
struggling with afflictions and burdens that are
almost impossible to bear.
May God grant to us the sensitivity to comprehend
something of what they are going through
and the urgency to demonstrate our concern for them
as we hold them up before God in prayer.

1 Thessalonians 3

We ought to spend much time in thanksgiving—
   for what God has done for us and for what
   He is doing through His beloved servants.
And we ought to rejoice and to praise our God—
   in advance—for what He will continue to do
   through His sons and daughters throughout
   the world about us.
We ought to have enough hindsight to see that the
   afflictions that plagued us and the conflicts that
   did beset us brought many of us closer to God and
   became the crucible that purified and fortified
   us for loving servanthood.
If we recognize God's dealings in our past—
   and this in spite of our failings and faithlessness—
   we should be encouraged to put our future in His hands
   and believe that God blesses through the storm
   and the static as well as through the sublime
   and the ecstatic.

Whatever our God allows in our lives is designed or
   can be utilized to enable us to increase and abound
   in love for one another and for our fellow persons
   all over our world, to establish, to sink deep our
   trust in Him, and to be ready for our Lord's return
   or for that hour when we shall return to Him.

1 Thessalonians 4

Whereas we need never to strive for our salvation,
    for God's forgiving love and acceptance,
    we need constantly to struggle and strive
    within the process of Christian growth.
It is the struggle to allow God to have His way with us:
    to cast off the shackles of self-concern,
    the appendages of fear and worry,
    our dependency upon the things of this earth, our
    fleshly desires for material security and recognition,
    our gnawing need to be successful,
    that we might be open and pliable, loose and flexible
    to the Spirit's indwelling and outpouring.
If we could truly abide in the Vine,
    we would grow and bear good fruit.
Our conflict lies in learning how to abide,
    to let go and let God, to rest in what He has done
    for us, and to be totally committed to Him
    and what He wants to do through us.

This means that we, using our God-given discernment,
    deny ourselves those things that endanger our
    relationship to God and come between us and the
    welfare of our fellow persons,
    that we shun those inborn lusts that dominate our
    attitudes and actions,
    and allow the transforming power of God's love to
    mold and shape us into the kind of vessels that
    He can use to perform His purposes.
We were not created to be gods unto ourselves—
    for self-seeking and self-serving;

we were created and redeemed to be the children of
the only true God, and we will find our supreme joy
only in His order and orbit for our lives.
It is by His grace and within His plan for our lives
that we learn how to truly love one another
and to live and work as God's servants
who really care about each other.

We need to be reminded that our earthly conflicts will
one day resolve in an eternal life and experience
that is more glorious than anything we can imagine.
Our dear ones who are no longer with us have
already entered into that experience.
It awaits every one of us who remains faithful to our Lord
and to His commission for us in our remaining
days upon this world.
Remember, Jesus died—and rose again.
So we shall rise again and,
with those who have preceded us,
be joined totally and eternally to our God and Christ.

1 Thessalonians 5

Over against those generous attempts of self-appointed
prophets to predict the visible return of our Lord
are our Lord's own words informing us that His return
or reappearance will be sudden and unexpected.
And yet the final coming of Christ should be
no surprise to His faithful disciples.
We ought to be ready to meet our Lord

whatever the appointed day or hour.
It really makes little difference whether we be alive
    or have already passed on to life everlasting;
    when He comes we shall see Him and with Him
    consummate His purposes in our world.

While we live upon this planet,
    we should live as if He were already here.
Indeed, He is here! He has come!
His disappearance after His resurrection was
    followed by Pentecost.
And Pentecost marked, in a wonderful event,
    His return to invisibly infill
    and indwell the hearts of His disciples.
The way in which we can always be ready for the final
    and ultimate reappearance of Christ
    is not to gather on some hill in pious meditation.
It is to recognize and rely
    upon the Spirit of God within us
    and to extend His kingdom
    through serving humanity about us.
We are to walk in faith, to serve in joy,
    and to praise God whatever the circumstances
    that surround us.
God grant that we may be totally His.
Then we are ever ready for His visible reappearance.

2 Thessalonians 1

While we thank our God for His loving patience
  in the face of our reluctance to grow,
  our slowness in maturing and developing into the
  kind of instruments that would be useful to Him,
  and praise Him for the comfort and security we
  find in Him even in the midst of this world's
  conflicts and calamities, we are disturbed by the
  cries of pain, the sounds of suffering,
  that break through into our hallowed little circle.
There is so much happening in our world that we
  can do very little about—
  and our verbal assurance that God loves His own
  appears to be as empty as wind in view of the
  oppression and deprivation that afflict
  multitudes of people in our own time.

God is righteous and just,
  and we cannot help but believe that the oppressors
  and deprivers of our world will ultimately come
  face to face with the stern judgment of God.
We forget, however, that judgment begins with us,
  that there may be some of us who are partly
  responsible for some of the horrendous things
  that are happening today,
  or that we are not doing all that we can within our
  commission and within the power God has made available
  to us to confound the oppressors or to relieve the
  suffering of our sisters and brothers in our
  community and world.
There are some people we cannot help at this moment—

and we prayerfully commit them to
the loving-kindness of God.
There are others that we can aid and sustain;
if we neglect to do all that we can to hold them
up or help share their suffering,
we ourselves may be subject to God's judgment.

Our thanksgiving must be thanks accompanied by giving—
the giving of ourselves to others in need—
or it may be little more than mockery.
It is relatively easy to condemn our world's oppressors
and relegate them to whatever hell God may have
prepared for them.
It is more difficult, but far more important,
that we lovingly and sacrificially identify with
the oppressed, that we share their afflictions and
stand with them against the monsters who use and
abuse them, and that we discover together the joy
and freedom of living for God.
If God is to "set at liberty those who are oppressed,"
He must do so through His servants on this planet.
And we are, thanks be to God, His servants.

2 Thessalonians 2 and 3

It is not surprising, in the darkness of this world's
chaotic struggles, that we hope intensely for the
very special intervention of God through the promised
return of our Lord, Jesus Christ.
We feel at times so unnerved, frightened, bowled over

with frustration and despair that we look desperately
for some sign in the sky, some miracle out of heaven,
and even wish for the final day of this dispensation,
the culmination of God's purposes upon this world
that will put an end to the misery
that abounds about us.
Nor is it surprising that many of us will grab at any
straw in the wind, latch on to any strange happening,
that may suggest the possibility of this
taking place in our lifetime.
Christians have been doing this for centuries,
and yet time marches on—and with it the sorrows
and joys of this world's inhabitants.
Maybe God is telling us to mind our own business—
to tend to those matters which He would have us to
be concerned about, to leave these cosmic, still
unknown and unrevealed things in His hands and,
while we accept His promises concerning the great
day of our total union with Him,
to occupy ourselves with the task at hand—
that of laboring within our suffering world to reveal
and communicate His love to all His human creatures.

We ought to be thankful that He saved, appointed, and
commissioned us for just such a time as this.
The world as it is at this moment is exactly where He
wants us to be.
He has entrusted us with the commission to represent
Him and reveal Him to this kind of world.
He is the only hope for mankind,
and we are the harbingers of that hope.
He is, and this is beyond our comprehension,
dependent upon His redeemed children to prepare
this world for the day of His appearing.

We obviously still have not completed that
    important assignment.
Let us be about it—and leave those things that
    need not be our ultimate concern up to Him.

The conditions of our world, the apostasy,
    the corruption, the utter disregard for God
    and His will, the atrocities and tragedies,
    and our failures in attempting to change the
    course of this world's rush to self-destruction
    drive us back to our God to be renewed and recharged,
    to be reassured and encouraged.
So be it, but God forbid that we end up thumb-twiddling
    on some high and holy hill to wait for His appearing.
If we do, we may be caught short;
    for He would thrust us out—again and again—
    into the tempests of our dark world to bring His
    light and love and salvation to the impoverished
    souls of fear-stricken men and women.

1 Timothy 1

Many of our friends have been led astray and betrayed
    by religious leaders, or by unqualified people
    brazenly assuming such positions, who promote a
    religion of Law and ethics under the banner
    of Christianity.
While these self-styled theologians may not be devious,
    they are in error and are propagating error.
They are polluting the pure Gospel of

God-revealed-through-Christ with the dangerous
ingredient of work-righteousness, and there are
respected people in our own camp who buy into their
product and unwittingly make it a part of their faith.
In a society where crime and corruption,
family breakdowns, and sexual promiscuity are on the
rise, in a nation where much-relied-on structures
are crumbling, it is indeed tempting to correlate
laws and rules and orders with the Gospel of love
and freedom that was proclaimed and demonstrated
by Jesus Christ.
We need to be guided, and sometimes inhibited,
by laws and rules.
It is when we make them a part of the Gospel we
proclaim and live by that we endanger our faith and
promote a system of beliefs that may corrupt
the faith of others.

Our salvation does *not* come,
nor is our relationship to God assured,
by our subscription to particular rules and orders,
be they traditional or contemporary,
that are being peddled as Gospel today.
We are saved by faith, by our total acceptance
of what Christ has done on our behalf,
by our commitment to God and His will for our lives.
The law is designed for the lawless;
some type of morality must be imposed upon the immoral;
order may be forced upon the disorderly;
but the sons and daughters of God are involved in
and directed by a far superior discipline, and that is
the love-God-love-your-fellow-persons directive
from the heart of God Himself, which is possible only
for those people who are recipients of,

and participants in, God's forgiving, saving love.
Even while we measure up to man-made laws and rules,
we are, apart from Christ, lawbreakers, sinners,
traitors to and enemies of God
and His eternal objectives.
It is as sinners that we are eligible for God's
saving love.
While we remain sinners perpetually drawing upon divine
forgiveness, we are the recipients of and channels
for God's love and are responsible for manifesting
a style of life and living that stands far above
the laws of our land.

1 Timothy 2 and 3

God's commission to His children concerns the
spiritual welfare of all men and women.
This means that God's will, our objective, is the
salvation of the whole human family.
We should, of course, offer our prayers to God
on behalf of, and extend our efforts to witness
in word and deed to, every human being—
from our leaders and executives in high places
to the laborer, the poor, the uneducated,
and the oppressed.
There is only one God, and that is the God
that Christ revealed.
This is the only God that we can worship and serve,
and we are the ministers of this God to the people
of our world.

Salvation does not come to us by way of the Law,
    but the accepting and propagating of God's love
    through Christ does impose upon us
    certain responsibilities.
We are to live through loving, and this requires that
    we be nonviolent, peaceful, kind, humble, tolerant,
    nonjudgmental, concerned, fairminded, self-giving,
    and persistent seekers for equality and dignity,
    freedom and opportunity, for every man and woman.
We need to be certain, as far as possible,
    that the leaders we select fulfill these requisites
    and that their lives promote by example the kind of
    character that will inspire and challenge
    their constituents.
Indeed, every one of us as God's ministers is expected
    to behave properly, not only in respect to
    society's laws, but in the reflection of God's eternal
    love for us and for all His created children.

1 Timothy 4

Everyone has the right to conduct his own affairs
    as he sees fit as long as his habits and activities
    do not stand between him and God or come between him
    and his fellow persons.
He may choose to be a vegetarian, a teetotaler,
    a bachelor; he may fast or abstain, chant or pray,
    light candles or wear a crucifix.
If he, however, assumes that these actions guarantee

his salvation, he is wrong;
if he promotes any such activities as necessary to
the sanctification of his fellow persons,
his is promoting a false gospel.
What may contribute to a person's physical health may
not necessarily contribute to his spiritual well-being.
While some people may abstain from eating meat
or drinking wine, others receive these things with
thanksgiving as the very gifts of God.
Much of what is construed as religion today is pure myth
and does little more than obscure the truth
and deceive those who would seek the truth.

We do, nevertheless, need to adopt a discipline
in order to grow in the faith provided
and demonstrated by Christ.
Our spirits lean toward lethargy;
our self-serving instincts tend to stifle
our love for our fellow persons;
our lives become dull and flat and ineffective
unless we return often to the Fountain of Life
for refreshment and renewal.
One person's discipline may not match or meet
the needs of another,
but we must discover what is helpful for us
in terms of maturing and sustaining our faith.
If the flexing or exercising of our physical muscles
is necessary to bodily health,
how much more the disciplined use of our spiritual
gifts to our growth as a Christian!
God gave us faith—
the faith that embraces His precious gifts.
We must hang on to it, nurture it,
and grow in the true faith that is now ours.

1 Timothy 5 and 6

If we love one another,
  we will certainly respect one another:
  the elderly who may be physically weak but mentally
  wise and strong;
  those who have lost their mates but not their love
  for their Lord and have so much to contribute
  to the kingdom of God;
  our spiritual leaders who, though human and fallible,
  are the custodians of certain gifts that are able
  to enrich our lives and guide us
  in our service to others;
  the laborer who works hard for his wages
  and certainly deserves what he receives;
  the employer who carries heavy responsibilities
  in directing and rewarding those who work under him;
  the teacher who gives unstintingly of herself
  to impart wisdom and good judgment to her pupils;
  our young people who may lack the wisdom
  but possess the energy and enthusiasm so necessary
  for Christian service;
  our mothers and fathers who put their lives and
  fortunes on the line in their concern for the physical
  and spiritual welfare of their offspring.
If we have the necessities of life,
  let us be content even if we cannot enjoy
  luxuries as others do.
There is no guarantee of happiness in the things of this
  world, and the people who think they find happiness
  in such are deluded and often thereby prevented from

discovering that true, eternal joy that comes to
us through God's gift of love.
We are commanded to renounce, to remain detached from,
the things of this world lest they hinder our
relationship to God and deter our commitment to
His objectives.

Our primary focus must be upon God and godliness,
Christ and Christian service,
and upon those attributes that become the consequence
of loving devotion to our Savior and Lord.
In the event that some of us are recipients
of material wealth,
we are also charged with a wealth of responsibility
to see to it, as the stewards of God, that His gifts
to us do not dilute our devotion to Him but
accentuate our commitment to the needs
of our brothers and sisters.
May God help us to guard carefully what has been
committed to us—not that we keep it for ourselves,
for then we only lose it—
but that we invest it wisely in the blessed task of
drawing others into the redeeming love of
our great God.

2 Timothy 1

Some of us, in our timidity or our feelings of
inferiority, almost give the appearance of being
ashamed of our faith.

126

We are threatened by today's intellectuals or
frightened by the hypotheses of our scientists,
or the theories of humanists and agnostics that appear
to contradict the blessed truths of God's Word as we
have been taught and as we have experienced them.
We may have earned the scorn of secular scholars by our
childish clutch upon the traditional symbols or the
ancient explanations of our faith, but our belief in
the one true God as revealed by Jesus Christ is
something we never need to be ashamed of.
God is our Creator, our Redeemer,
and the source of all the grace and power we need
to live happy, contributive lives.
We can proclaim and, even more important, demonstrate
the grace and power of this great God by claiming
our freedom from the fears and anxieties,
the temporal and materialistic bondages of this world,
to love and serve our fellow persons in joy.
We know, not by the fallible tests and explorations
of scientists but by personal experience,
that we are the sons and daughters of God and that we
have been commissioned to be His ministers of
His saving love to all who will listen and respond.

Rather than respond, however, many people will react
skeptically or violently to our witness and style
of life, and this may result in pain and suffering
for the servants of God.
It need not result in the loss of our faith.
We have God's promise that He watches over His own
and nothing can take them away from Him.
In the event that we feel our confidence shaken
or our faith threatened,
whether such is due to the sufferings that afflict us

or the persuasive speech of false prophets that
confounds us, we must return to the words
and promises of our Lord to regain strength
and courage to carry on our ministry.

2 Timothy 2

Suffering is to be expected in the course of our
life and ministry.
It is an integral part of any course of life
in our world.
Laborers, professional persons, dedicated artists,
political leaders must all endure times of suffering
and hardship if they are truly dedicated to their
respective callings.
Even the ordinary and important task of rearing
a family involves suffering.
Is it so unusual or unthinkable that the ministers of God
be expected to endure suffering as they serve amongst
suffering people in a suffering world?
Be reminded of Jesus Christ—
and what He suffered on our behalf.
Perhaps it is His suffering that is being extended
through us when we endure sorrow and pain
in the process of bringing Christ to others.
At any rate, we have His promise that as we suffer and
endure for His sake so we shall truly discover the
joy of living, that out of the ashes of our suffering
and dying comes the beauty of life everlasting.

We have nothing to lose but everything to gain as we
    suffer in our walk with God and in our
    service to humanity.
And God will grant us the grace to endure and even
    to grow and mature through our suffering.
As a mother discovers in her newborn child a joy
    that almost obliterates any memory of the very real
    and intense pangs that preceded the birth of that
    child, so we who minister as the servants of God
    discover out-of-this-world joys that crowd out the
    memories of pain and suffering.
The conflicts of the past,
    whether those battles were won or lost,
    fade into hazy, indistinct recollections as we bask
    in the incredible and indescribable joys of being the
    ministers of God in our pain-ridden world.
Do we need to be reminded that the God who gives us joy
    is always with us in our sufferings?

In respect to suffering, there are some things that the
    sons and daughters of God do not have to suffer.
We do not have to suffer over past sins—
    though the consequences of such may haunt us at times.
Christ has suffered on our behalf and has granted
    us His forgiveness.
Nor do we have to suffer fear, or bow down under failure,
    or feel that our lives are wasted.
We are engaged in the greatest vocation granted to God's
    creatures—that of serving Him through our loving
    service to our fellow creatures.
It is worth everything we have to give to it—
    this appointment under God.
Even the sufferings, the conflicts, the crucible
    experiences that prepare us to be God's ministers

of love are worth enduring if they better equip us
for His assignment before us.
We need not pray that God remove our painful experiences,
but that He transform them into cleansing fires that
renew and refurbish us for His purposes,
and that we always remain faithful to Him.

2 Timothy 3 and 4

We live in a world that appears to be rapidly
sliding downhill.
Things seem to be getting worse rather than better.
And this is in spite of the countless Christians
who are faithfully serving God and man in their
respective posts in every nation on this globe.
It may be because there are more people now or that so
many of their bizarre activities are reported through
the world-embracing media of our day,
but there appears to be more pride and hate
and rebelliousness and ingratitude and violence
and prejudice and self-serving than ever before.
We are not to fall into the same cesspools of iniquity
as do so many out of the multitudes about us,
but we are to live and serve amongst those multitudes.
At the risk of life and limb,
of property and possessions,
we are to proclaim and reflect and demonstrate God
as revealed through Christ.

We cannot hide away in holy sanctuaries.
As Christ descended into our chaos—lived and died
    in the midst of our madness—
    so we are to reflect the love and sanity
    of God's will and order in our insane world.
How else can God's saving love for mankind be revealed
    except through His redeemed children
    now upon this planet?
This is our assignment; this is our sphere of activity.
There is no guarantee that people will respond
    to the Gospel that we preach.
We already know from experience that many
    will discredit our efforts and deny our God
    and even persecute His servants.
We are, nevertheless, commanded to preach, exhort,
    convince, to pull from the dark waters those who
    are perishing, like brands from the fire those who
    are burning, that those out of the multitudes who
    are still capable of seeking for something more than
    the material and the sensual may be ready to return to
    their Creator and discover in Him their blessed
    redemption made possible through Jesus Christ.

Our task is not to convert or change the people
    to whom we witness.
We are to reveal a loving God, a living Christ,
    to these people through our verbal witnessing
    and our loving concern.
God will take it from there—and many out of this
    world's multitudes will be brought back to the
    heart of God and know the joy that we have found and
    daily experience as His children and ministers.

Titus 1, 2, and 3

Laws and rules, rituals and spiritual disciplines will
    not win God's favor or make us acceptable to Him.
Christ has fulfilled the Law on our behalf.
God's forgiving and saving love becomes applicable to us
    in that moment that we make it our own through faith.
Nevertheless, our sincere and total commitment to any
    goal demands character and discipline.
So, too, our commitment to God and His purposes requires
    a commitment which becomes synonymous with faith.

What about our commitment, and the kind of character
    and discipline that will help us to grow in the faith
    and to demonstrate that faith to our fellow persons?
We must, as individuals, find our own level in respect
    to the life-style that will best enrich our faith
    and serve God's purposes in our arena of activity.

There are, however, requirements or expectations that
    apply to all of us as the ministers of God.
We must cease to be self-serving materialists,
    the accumulators of things, and to put our concern
    for the needs of our fellow persons on par with our
    own wants and needs.
We must control our inner urges, instincts,
    and frustrations that may cause harm to our
    fellow persons and hinder or limit our witness of
    love to them.
We must be immersed in and faithful propagators of
    the doctrines of our faith as revealed in the life
    and teachings of Jesus Christ.

We are, whether we like it or not, on stage and are
  bearing witness concerning our loving God by our
  daily lives, our actions and deeds,
  as much as by the things that we may say.
This doesn't warrant prissy and Pollyannaish attitudes,
  or a system of morality that has little to do with
  truly loving people and may, in effect,
  turn away our peers from our witness.
We must, of course, be sober, temperate, steadfast,
  and dedicated.
We are to deny ourselves those things which may be
  harmful to ourselves or to others.
We are to respect our authorities and to be obedient
  to those laws that benefit our society.
We are to be nonjudgmental, to speak evil of no one,
  to avoid scandal or scandalizing and destructive
  criticizing or quarreling.
Bigotry or prejudice has no place whatsoever
  in our lives.
We are not to give in to envy, covetousness,
  jealousy, or malice.
We are to be kind, considerate, constructive,
  known and trusted as those who speak and stand up
  for the truth, for equality, dignity, and opportunity
  for every human being, and who resist and denounce
  the oppression and exploitation of people
  anywhere in our world.
We are to commit ourselves to loving and doing that which
  is of benefit and value to the human family.
We are to be everything our Lord was in His days
  upon this planet and what He would have us to
  be as His servants in our century.
This is a large order,

an almost frightening responsibility,
and is possible only by the grace of God.
We are challenged to claim that grace and truly live
like the sons and daughters of our great and loving
God.

Philemon

Our relationship to our fellow human beings within the
body of Christ is of paramount importance.
Our roles as the ministers of Christ,
our assignments as His beloved servants
may greatly vary.
Some of us are leaders who have been granted a position
of authority over others.
We ought to be aware that our social or educational
status, regardless of what it means to our peers,
does not impress our Lord;
every one of His children is equally important to Him.
And we need to be reminded, from time to time,
that with leadership comes responsibility,
the responsibility to treat those who work under
us as our equals before God, and to love them as such,
our brothers and sisters in Christ.

We are, every one of us, the ministers of God.
There are those who serve God even in the process
of serving us.
They are those who make it possible for us to fulfill
our responsibilities in our arena of service.

We need each other, parent and child,
employer and employee, master and servant.
We must, together, submit to the Master of masters,
the Lord of lords, our Redeemer and King,
our Father and our God.
Together we seek to fulfill His objectives and advance
His kingdom upon our world.
We do so as members of the same family,
the family of God and Christ.

Hebrews 1

Our great God did, of course, reveal something
of Himself and His plan for His human creatures
to our Hebrew forefathers.
Whereas they may not have been ready
for the ultimate revelation,
they did perceive a holy and righteous God
with infinite concern for His covenanted people.
We, however, are the children of God to whom He has
revealed His loving acceptance of us through
His Son, Jesus Christ.
We could not reach up to God, so magnificent and
unattainable His holiness and righteousness;
so he reached down to us.
Our God, whom we could not see or hear or touch,
broke out of His spiritual dimension to enter our
three-dimensional world in order to speak and
deal with us directly, proclaiming and demonstrating
His eternal love to His human creatures.

We have no way of comprehending the magnitude of
    His great sacrifice, but He became one of us,
    descending from His great heights of glory to
    plunge into our chaotic bungling, and this in order
    to embrace us and draw us back to Himself.
He did this by way of sending us His Son, Jesus Christ,
    who subjected Himself to all of the conditions of
    our morality, submitting even to the power and
    authority of corrupted, self-serving, misguided men,
    that He might become the way and life and truth
    for all who seek to be related to their God.

It is God as revealed through this Christ whom we
    worship and serve today.
It is only through this Christ and what He has done
    on our behalf that we can find our way back to God
    and become His truly beloved children and servants.
Praise God for Jesus Christ,
    God's Revealer and our Redeemer!

Hebrews 2

The revelation of God has been adequate.
We know all that we need to know, have seen all that
    we need to see, can experience all that we need
    to experience, to be assured of God's saving love.
There is no longer any excuse for our ignorance
    or our reluctance to return to our Creator and God,
    and those who procrastinate have no one to
    blame but themselves.

God has come to us—assuming a status and a position
that was inferior to the very angels who were His
subordinates—becoming mortal, taking upon Himself
our very nature, born of a human mother, died at
the hands of cruel executioners, all in order that
we might live forever as His sons and daughters.
And He continues to dwell with us—through His Spirit
who inhabits our lives, reveals His purposes,
and provides His grace for joyful and meaningful
living and serving.
Indeed, there is no excuse, and there is no other way
into the loving heart of God.

What a Savior we have!
We are no longer strangers to God, aliens to His love
and holiness, traitors to His purposes.
Jesus actually became, in spiritual terms, our Brother.
He participated in our humanity, identified with
our sufferings, shared in our weaknesses,
and He called us His brothers and sisters.
We can't fathom this amazing truth; but we can become,
with Christ, God's sons and daughters by participating
in and becoming identified with this Christ
and His revelations of the Father.
Through Christ we now have the same Father;
with Christ we become His beloved children.
It happens the very moment we claim and lay hold of
and submit to, by faith, what God through Christ
has done on our behalf.

Hebrews 3

Jesus truly is our Brother, but He is so much more.
Whereas we love and we share as siblings,
    we glorify our Brother Jesus as God's beloved Son,
    our Redeemer, our Lord, as One with God in the very
    creation of our universe, and as far more important
    to us than any past prophet, apostle, gifted teacher
    or preacher of this or any other century.
Therefore, it is when we hear His voice,
    as we have heard and will hopefully continue to
    hear it, that we had better take notice.
Our salvation is dependent upon a true faith
    in what Christ has done on our behalf,
    the kind of faith that expresses itself
    not only in vocal profession,
    but also in loving obedience
    to His proclamations and commands.

We know what happened to our forebears who deliberately
    or carelessly fell short of God's commandments
    and standards.
God speaks to us through Jesus Christ and His
    ever-present Spirit in our lives.
It is quite possible that we, too, may fail to hear His
    Word or may foolishly ignore His will for our lives.
Our relationship to God, our inclusion in His family,
    is effected and sustained by faith.
That faith is to be demonstrated in our
    ever-deepening commitment to God and His purposes.
It is very difficult to go solo in respect to our
    daily relationship to God.

Not only do we continue to rely upon God's grace;
　　we need each other's help, and we need to love,
　　share, struggle with, and support one another
　　in our walk with God.

Hebrews 4

The good news of the Gospel—of our great God lovingly
　　reaching down to us through Jesus Christ—
　　has come to us; we have heard it again and again.
But hearing the Good News, our exposure to the
　　proclamation of the Gospel, does not guarantee its
　　reception and its experience in our hearts and lives.
Our whole country and most of our world have heard
　　and continue to hear through one media-form or
　　another the Good News of God's saving grace.
Yet we may well assume that relatively few out of our
　　world's masses know what it really means to be
　　received into the family of God.
As a hungry man with a million dollars in his bank
　　account can starve to death simply because he hasn't
　　heard of his bonus or refuses to believe in his
　　good fortune, so there are multitudes today who are
　　spiritually dying—starving to death—because,
　　even if they have heard, they are not able or willing
　　to believe that the God who created them stands ready
　　to redeem them and grant them eternal life.

That man who, by faith, enters into the life and grace
　　granted by God is introduced to a life of

joy and peace and rest.
He ceases his fruitless struggles to please or win
the favor of his Creator and rests in what God
through Christ has already done for him.
He enters, as well, a whole new vocation for his life,
for while he rests in God's loving-kindness,
he begins to labor in a new dimension as a son and
servant of God to introduce others to the life of
eternal joy and rest that is available to them
through Jesus Christ.

We need to renew, to charge up our faith from
time to time, to make sure we keep the faith,
lest we back out on our relationship to God and
fall once more into that fruitless struggle to exist
apart from God.
We have, in our Lord, Jesus Christ, not only a Savior,
but a Keeper, a Guardian over our souls,
One who knows our failings and hang-ups,
who understands the trials and conflicts that come
our way, and who will grant us the grace to come
through them unscathed.
There will be wounds, and scars that remind us of
those wounds, but victory is assured if we stay close
to that One who is the dispenser of divine grace.

Hebrews 5

In the days of our forefathers high priests
were appointed to stand between a sinful people

and a holy God, to act on behalf of the people.
These priests, appointed by their peers,
    were themselves sinners
    and could therefore understand the frailties
    and weaknesses of the children of Israel
    for whom, through sacrifices and ceremonies,
    they sought God's forgiveness.
In Christ we honor the Priest of all priests, who has
    been assigned by God Himself to present the Sacrifice
    of sacrifices—His own body upon the cross—
    as sufficient to atone for all the sins of
    all people in all the world.
Knowing their weakness without succumbing to weakness,
    tempted without yielding to temptation,
    Jesus is our worthy Advocate in reconciling
    forgiven sinners with a forgiving God.
And yet some of us act at times as if the price Jesus
    paid is insufficient to cover our guilt.
If we are assigned to be ministers of God,
    how dare we be contented with the Pablum of
    work-righteousness, or the sweet honey of subjective
    ecstasy, the milk of cloud-hopping experiences, when
    we ought by now to be feeding on the solid meat
    of Christ's radical, risk-fraught, joy-giving
    teachings and activities?
God help us to grow up in the Christian life,
    to mature, to develop some sensitivity to the needs
    of people and some skill in terms of applying the
    life and doctrines of Christ to those needs.
We are God's ministers;
    may He make us worthy of our appointment.

Hebrews 6

There are many within our religious institutions today
    who are loyal to their particular symbols and
    disciplines but whose faith in God is about as
    authentic as that of the agnostic humanists and
    social reformers they so avidly condemn.
Some are playing games with God;
    they are wheeler-dealers seeking to satiate their
    aesthetic needs apart from genuine commitment to
    the God they presume to worship.
Others have never emerged from the Sunday school
    comprehensions, the Lord-is-my-Shepherd presentations,
    that serve to warm and comfort, assure and protect
    them in a violent, unstable world.
And because they don't grow up in the faith, they remain
    stunted, retarded, ineffective as the ministers and
    servants of God, dangerously locked into their little
    saved-by-faith, second-coming, gifts-of-the-Spirit
    cubbyholes while the real sons and daughters of God
    are out risking their possessions and their lives
    on the front lines of our Lord's great enterprise.
Of course we are saved by faith—
    but we are also saved for hazardous
    and sacrificial service to our fellow persons.
We affirm the eventual visible reappearance of our Lord—
    and the gifts of the Spirit;
    we also insist that the time of Christ's appearance
    and the administration of the Spirit's gifts are
    the responsibility of God, and our charge is to accept
    our appointment as His disciples and concentrate
    on carrying out His purposes.

We do not disavow or grow away from the basic principles
of our faith.
We repeatedly reaffirm and celebrate them.
We need, constantly, to return to God's great promises
of life and salvation, of His eternal love and
ever-present concern for His children.
It is this that ought to resolve in joyful obedience
to His will for us—in the assurance that our gains
will be far greater than our losses as we commit
ourselves to His service in our world.

Hebrews 7 and 8

The basic tenet, the principal cornerstone of our
Christian experience,
is God's total acceptance of us through Jesus Christ.
There may be some people who can be genuinely altruistic
and self-giving apart from the knowledge
and experience of God's love and acceptance,
but we who have returned to God through Christ
and who know God as our Father and Christ as
our Brother would find most of our motives
for self-sacrificing service crumbling into rubble
if this knowledge and experience were taken away
from us.
It is thus that we need to recognize continually
the glorious truth that Jesus once and for always
reconciled us to His Father and our God.
Before the appearance of our Savior and Christ

143

people found it necessary to fill the spiritual
    vacuum in their lives by creating their own gods
    that they could see and worship or by appointing
    some sort of high priest who could stand between
    them and the invisible, intangible God.
Whereas they did what they had to do under the
    circumstances and kept their search for their God
    alive through their efforts, we have been chosen
    to discover and relate to the true God through the
    coming of His own Son into our world.
He is our great, one-and-only High Priest, who broke
    through every barrier between man and God and
    revealed Him as a forgiving, loving, grace-giving God.
We no longer need to lean on symbols or rely on priests
    to make God real and available to us.
He has been revealed through Jesus Christ.
The act of reconciliation has been effected through
    His sacrificial death and supernatural resurrection
    on our behalf.
God continues to reveal Himself through His Spirit
    in and through the activities and proclamations of
    those who follow this Christ.

Jesus did what no mortal priest or religious leader
    can ever do—obliterated the darkness,
    the uncertainty, and the inscrutability that once
    existed between God and man, and restored us forever
    to an intimate relationship with Him.
Everything that happened before Christ was but a shadow
    of what was to come, even those truth-seeking attempts
    at worship that prepared the way for the coming Christ.
Christ is the truth that has come and is here
    in Spirit to draw men and women to the truth.
He is the way to God—directly and eternally.

He is the life that perpetually sustains us and compels
 us to dedicate our lives to broadcasting this truth
 to those who are still in darkness.
He is the fulfillment of our deepest longings,
 the answer to our most complex problems.
He is Christ, our Lord, our God, and our Way to God.

Hebrews 9 and 10

We are aware of the innumerable and often impossible
 rituals and regulations that encompassed
 the religion of our forefathers.
Their routines of worship, the officiants who served in
 those rituals, the times and modes of dress, the
 activities of those who sought their God at such
 times and in such places, were carefully observed.
Even at that, there was more hope for, than assurance of,
 God's acceptance of the activities of those people
 who sought genuinely for God's favor in the only
 manner that they knew.
It was largely centered about priests and animal
 sacrifices, the need for someone to mediate between
 man and God and the need for blood offerings to
 substitute for, or be offered as, just payment
 for man's sin.
We are unable to determine just what value
 these activities were to those ancient worshipers,
 but they do have value to us in that, amazingly,
 they provide a basis for understanding the great

redemption of man that was to come—
the redemption that is ours through Jesus Christ.
The worshipers of ancient Israel assumed that the
obstacles between God and man were almost
insurmountable, thus the inner and outer sanctuaries,
the Holy of Holies, the specially appointed
high priests, the blood offerings, all aiming to
ferret out God's mercy in the face of
man's frailties and failings.
Jesus, our great High Priest, entered the Holy of Holies,
the inner sanctum of God, giving His life as the one,
sufficient, perfect sacrifice to end all sacrifices,
in order to make men and women holy, righteous,
and totally acceptable to His heavenly Father.
What the ancient law and religious orders could not do
God did on man's behalf through His Son, Jesus Christ.
The forgiveness of God is complete, canceling out the
necessity of any future offerings or sacrifices.

It is for this reason and because of what Christ has
done for us that we have the assurance and confidence
that we need, to boldly approach our loving God.
And we can come before God with untroubled consciences,
knowing that our past sins will no longer
be held against us.
We are now the people of God,
His children and servants forever.

It becomes important, however, that we who have by faith
entered with Christ into the Holy of Holies keep that
faith and allow nothing to deter us in our walk of
faith and obedience.
It is worth whatever cost we may have to pay—
the loss of our jobs, reputations,

material possessions, even the sacrifice of our lives—
that we hold fast our salvation and follow closely
behind our Lord.
And this we will do—with the help of God.

Hebrews 11

Faith, "the assurance of things hoped for,
    the conviction of things not seen," is already an
    integral part of our everyday lives.
We can't even reach for a breath of air without a
    measure of faith.
Whether we eat or drink, drive or shop, walk across the
    street or deposit our money in a bank,
    we must have faith.
We simply cannot exist apart from faith.
It is faith that becomes the essential ingredient in
    the appropriation of God's infinite blessings.
There is a long roster, from the beginning of Israel's
    history to this very day, of men and women who found
    and followed the teachings and directions of their
    God in faith.
Often against almost insurmountable odds, these splendid
    saints demonstrated their complete confidence in God's
    Word to them—committing their very lives to the
    proposition that God is God and His Word is truth
    and the accomplishment of His purposes the most
    important thing in the world.

The faith we utilize in our daily lives becomes

habitual and almost automatic.

The faith that is required by God entails a total
commitment to His Word and objectives and involves
a concentration upon, and a dedication to, His plan
for people's lives that demands the utmost
that God's human creatures can give.

Indeed, the very God who demands faith must give to
men and women the faith that He demands.

It all begins with a belief in the existence of God.

This is a beginning, but it is not sufficient for
man's salvation.

It grows, and this usually through or because of people
who care about us, into a conviction concerning God's
love for His creatures, and more particularly,
His love for us as individuals.

Whatever the ancient believers may have understood
about God, and some of them did receive some very
special revelations, they probably knew little
about His love;
yet they were aware of His righteous judgment
and dedicated their lives to obeying Him out of
both fear and faith.

We who are so amazed at the degree of their beliefs
have no excuse not to respond to God's love as it
is fully revealed in Jesus Christ.

If they dared to risk their lives for God as they
understood Him, how much more ought we to be willing
to manifest our confidence in, and commit our lives
to, God as He made Himself known to us through Christ!

Our great God has given to us the ability to have faith.

It is necessary for us to utilize and exercise this
ability, which is usually expended upon the finite
securities and relationships of this life;

to focus it upon the infinite grace of a loving God;
to accept His forgiving love as made applicable
through Christ and proclaimed through His Word; and,
in scorn of consequences,
to put our lives and fortunes in His hands.
Without faith there is no way of relating to God.
With faith, and its resultant commitment to Christian
discipleship,
there is joy and meaning,
risk and excitement, love and freedom,
purpose and objective as the very sons and
daughters of God.

Hebrews 12

Faith is in itself a gift of God.
It is not something we can manufacture.
And yet, one of our most powerful incentives,
and a means by which God grants to us the need and
the motivation to have faith and trust,
to believe in His gracious promises,
is the faith of those who have gone before us.
It ought to be enough to enable us to cut loose from
our inordinate attachment to earthbound securities,
to cast off our foolish doubts, and to let go,
let God, and let the chips fall where they may.
While our Lord is no longer visibly present,
we have His Word and His example to imitate
and to mature our faith.

There is, of course, an element of risk, a measure of
    pain involved in our walk of faith.
If we expect only sweetness and light,
    thrills and ecstasies as the consequences of our
    involvement with God and His purposes, we either
    have no faith whatsoever or have only an ephemeral
    relationship that may be eradicated by the
    traumatic events of our world.
Faith does not shield us from the episodes that wound
    us or the failures that flatten us in despair.
But faith is capable of embracing suffering and despair
    and molding and maneuvering them into instruments that
    mature us and make us more sensitive to the hurts of
    others even while we learn how to more graciously
    accept the difficulties and hardships of this life.
Rather than folding and floundering in the midst of
    every turbulence that engulfs us,
    we learn how to stand firm against the storm and walk
    steadily amongst the vicissitudes of daily living.
God is not some distant and indulgent Being;
    He is with us and within us seeking to work out
    His purposes through us.
Nor is He some fantasy that we can put handles on and
    manipulate in the direction of our needs and wants.
He is God—not One whom we can touch—
    but One in whom we can trust and are enabled to obey.
That is the God that we celebrate,
    One who stands over and above the frailties of His
    creatures and the atrocities of this world,
    yet able to advance His kingdom with us and through us
    by means of, or in spite of, the frailties
    and atrocities that plague us.
This is the God that we worship while being forever

amazed and gratified that our worship
is acceptable to Him.

Hebrews 13

We must guard carefully our relationships with
    one another and regard even those who are unknown
    to us as possible emissaries from God.
Every interpersonal relationship is a sacred trust—
    especially those within the family of faith.
We need to remember our comrades who are facing problems
    and conflicts that are even more severe than our own.
Our leaders, as human and frail and error-prone
    as we are, need our respect and our prayers.
When they are compelled to make unpopular decisions that
    are necessary to God's purposes, let us contribute
    to their courage and strength
    by giving them our support.
We are to do this joyfully, not fearfully,
    for we are all God's ministers and must learn
    how to suffer and rejoice together.
We are all God's emissaries to one another—and the
    means by which He shares His grace with the
    members of Christ's body.
Together we can march through a hostile world as the
    men and women of God—reaching out to the wanderers
    and stragglers by the way to draw them
    into God's family.
There will be a price to pay and pains to bear, but we
    will be able to handle them because we have a great

God whose love for us never changes and who
promises that eternal joy which we even now have
found in some measure and shall experience fully
and eternally when our march has been completed.

James 1

We have much to learn as the children of God.
The most difficult, perhaps, is to learn
    how to regard our trials and tribulations—
    even the tragedies that beset us—
    as capable of enhancing and enriching our lives.
Whereas God does not send them, He does permit them,
    and He can use them to draw us closer to Him
    and thereby accomplish His purposes
    in and through us.
We desperately need the wisdom to accept these
    painful happenings with graciousness, even with joy,
    knowing that whatever they may be,
    God can transform them from ugliness into beauty,
    from the plots of Satan designed to destroy
    into the purposes of God
    destined to do us good.
The key is a genuine faith in a loving God,
    a faith that frees us and strengthens us
    to endure whatever may come our way.

These tribulations do not come from God.
The conflicts we engage in have their origin in the
    forces of evil that permeate our hemisphere

as well as in our own self-centered natures,
the rebel will that recoils from the vision of light
and freedom and sacrificial love.
We won't win every battle in this incessant war
against the powers of the night,
but the ultimate victory is,
in Jesus Christ, already ours.
If we fall only to rise again, fail only to fight again,
we discover a forgiving and loving God
indwelling our hearts and strengthening our arms
to carry on this war of the ages.
It is not difficult to see or imagine God's presence
in sunlight and success,
but it is when we recognize that God is with us
in the crucible of conflict
that we experience real joy.

Let us be aware, however,
that we can be trapped by tribulation.
If we attempt to fight our selfish, sin-ridden desires
by ourselves, we are in for defeat
and eventual destruction.
Courting those inner fires
usually resolves in getting burned.
Faith in God and in His truth and grace
will give us the edge, and the final victory,
even over our enflamed passions and foolish errors.

There is something else we must learn as God's children.
It is not enough to be listeners and proclaimers
of the Gospel;
we are commissioned to be doers.
Christian faith that falls short of loving performance
in respect to the needs of suffering people about us

falls far short of genuine faith.
May our small faith be rekindled and burn bright
with joy and obedience.

James 2

It may seem like a small matter,
but it translates as a gigantic flaw in the lives
of scores of Christians.
They dare to call themselves believers in
and followers of Jesus Christ,
and yet they act like outright bigots in their
relationships to people who cross their path.
If we look carefully—and honestly—
we may recognize this to be one of our problems,
that we are among those who talk limitlessly about
loving humanity but who are really very selective
about whom we accept as the objects
of our love and concern.
It may be expected that we be very particular about
whom we live with and confide in,
but when we show greater respect for those who are
of our race or economic status
than we do for those who are not,
we are making distinctions
that our Lord will not make.

We are enjoined to love our neighbor as ourselves.
When our judgment of people or our actions toward them
are determined by the color of their skin,

the cut of their clothes,
or the size of their bank account,
we are not acting like the children
and servants of God—
and we ought to be ashamed of ourselves.
Indeed, we are sinning against God
and endangering our relationship to Him
when we neglect to give equal respect and value
to all of His children around us.
We need to reexamine our concepts of morality,
to blast out some of the silly notions that determine
our responses to life and people,
and learn how to be loving and compassionate.

Some of us are still hooked on that ridiculous notion
that religious faith is something to be exercised
mainly through the rituals of a worship service.
We may not admit it,
but the facts speak for themselves.
We are all mouth—in terms of testimonials—
but the rest of our bodies are often paralyzed
by unbelief or disobedience.
Whatever the reason—fear or apathy or selfishness—
or the possibility that we haven't yet really
embraced God's love,
what we are demonstrating
is a far cry from Christian faith.
We need to call a spade a spade,
to tear away the window dressing,
the fictitious labels,
and have the courage to confront the painful truth
that we can't talk faith unless we have faith.
And when we have the faith
that Jesus proclaimed and demonstrated,

we, in turn, will live it and demonstrate it
in sacrificial love for the human family about us.

Let us stop playing games with God,
accepting only what suits our selfish concepts,
and embrace Him as His Word declares Him to be.
Let us serve Him by serving our fellow person.

James 3

Some of us are endowed with particular gifts and are
therefore called to special positions of
responsibility within God's kingdom.
There must be preachers and teachers and spiritual
leaders in the Christian community.
If we are such, we need to be aware more than anyone
else that, not only will we make mistakes, but,
because of our high calling, they may be more serious
in their consequences and effects upon the community
about us.
Nevertheless, we are all the ministers of Christ, and
we have received from Him the authority and the tools
to carry out our ministry.
Whereas we must be concerned about our actions—
and they may be more expressive than anything we
can say—our speech, the words we utter, are of
tremendous importance.
They have an impact upon our interpersonal relationships
that is far greater than the energy involved in
speaking those words.

We must speak softly and carefully and, in many cases,
   only after we have listened intently.
Our words have the power to destroy.
A small leak can lead to the flooding of a large city;
   a little spark may set a forest on fire;
   the wrong word in the wrong place is capable of
   bringing darkness and division into the hearts
   of trusting people.
On the other hand, the right word at the right time
   can put a bit of heaven into the hell that afflicts
   the lives of countless people.
Thus the tongue that forms our words may be an instrument
   of God or a tool of the devil, a vehicle of love or
   the instigator and perpetuator of hatred;
   it can endear us to our fellow persons or drive a wedge
   between us, enrich our community or divide it asunder.

As a spring of water has a source—be it bitter or pure—
   so the flow of words whose source is the mind
   and heart of man and woman.
It is when our lives are centered upon God—
   bathed in love and dedicated to His purposes—
   that the words we speak and the actions that we take
   reach out to bless rather than destroy and produce
   healing and strength, light and joy to the spiritually
   maimed, the suffering, and those who walk in darkness.
May God teach us how to speak and act wisely,
   not out of the ambition of self-seeking and serving,
   but out of the joy and grace and peace of God's
   Spirit within us.

James 4

There is a war of sorts being waged within us which,
   if not adequately handled,
   is capable of creating a war around us.
It is initiated by the inner urge for self-gratification
   and glorification.
There seems always to be something on the inside that
   rebels against and attempts to dethrone the God
   who created us and claims us for Himself.
More often than not, we yield to those self-serving
   instincts and desires and thereby crowd the Spirit
   of God into some small corner of our lives wherein
   His influence and control upon us and through us
   is severely limited.
This inner force, when unleashed, is capable of turning
   us into the very enemies of God—of rupturing
   our faith and drawing us back into darkness again.
We cannot totally escape the siren calls of the
   natural man, and we shall always fall prey to those
   destructive powers when we do battle on their own
   ground.
We can, however, resist these urges and instincts,
   and resist them successfully if we do so with
   the grace that God grants to His children.
This grace He grants to those of us who submit to His
   loving intervention in our lives and who give Him
   permission to conquer and divide, control and remold
   our passions into vessels for His holy use.

Recognizing our own inner weaknesses,
   we are less likely to judge one another or to

say those things that may harm another person.
Acknowledging our own humanity, we will not be so apt
   to play God with our own lives,
   or toy with the emotions and affections of another.
Committed to God and His purposes, we will allow Him
   to design our destinies—and we will give Him the
   credit for those good things that He does accomplish
   through us.
It still hasn't occurred to many religious people that
   immorality not only characterizes the hurt they cause
   their fellow persons, but describes their failures
   to carry out those things that would bring blessing
   and benefit to people about them.
God grant that we continue to be human—
   acknowledging our frailties and failures—and yet
   authentic in our persistent search for, and acceptance
   of, God's control of our lives and destinies.

James 5

When we compare our good fortune with that of the
   major part of this world's population,
   we discover that many of us are wealthy
   in respect to the goods of this world.
Over against this disturbing revelation are the words
   of our Lord which identify the poor as the
   inheritors of the riches of heaven,
   and they suggest that the worldly wealthy will find
   it almost impossible to reach that heaven at all.

Our salvation comes only by God's grace;
when it does come, something happens to our riches.
Instead of possessors of this world's wealth,
we become its stewards and distributors,
redeemed and appointed by our Lord to carefully
invest this world's resources in the physical and
spiritual needs of our fellow persons throughout
the world.

Some of us are honestly trying to live up to our
Lord's requisites in respect to His gifts to us—
our talents and our worldly possessions.
Even when we do have the courage to break through our
selfishness and make daring investments in the welfare
of our fellow persons, we may see little or nothing
in terms of returns on our investments.
It may be that we never will—in this life.
Perhaps it is better that way.
If our sacrifices brought tangible returns,
they would cease to be sacrifices.
If faith is life in scorn of consequences, this kind of
faith ought also to be manifest in our good works.
The recipients of God's eternal riches should be able
to distribute their worldly goods without any concern
for rewards in this life or the next.
This is what love is all about.
God help us to lay hold of the freedom
that is ours in Christ.
Without grumbling or judging,
worrying or even wondering overmuch,
let us cut loose from these chains that bind us
to our earthbound natures and interests;
and let us learn how to float free—
to haphazardly risk our lives, possessions,

reputations, or whatever—for God and His purposes,
the human family and its needs,
and to do so without concern for consequences.
This may be the way to real happiness
in the kingdom of God.
Knowing the human condition,
it is probable that few of us will discover it.

We can help one another to discover this joyous
freedom in Christ.
We need to sing together, pray together,
bear one another's burdens,
be open and honest about our failures,
forgive one another, share in the other's sufferings,
support one another in our weaknesses,
and in all ways carry on together like the family
we are—the sons and daughters of God.

1 Peter 1

Another way to test whether or not our faith is genuine
is to see whether we can be thankful in the midst of
trying circumstances.
Some of us suffer much in the course of our lives.
All of us are continually exposed to temptations
and tribulations that are more than we can endure.
What we must understand is that God is able to use
even these things,
the apparently unfortunate happenings that hound us,
to accomplish His purposes in and through us.

We need only consult our memory banks to confirm
how even the tragedies that shafted us in the past
have made significant contributions to our lives
and made us more lovingly sensitive to
the sorrows and pains that befall others.
The key to strength and courage, the ability to endure,
and the grace to find beauty and joy even within
the crucible experiences of our lives is faith.
And faith is demonstrated and expressed when we
dare to be thankful, to shout God's praises,
even in the middle of our problems and pressures.

It is probable that we will be forcefully separated
from many people and things that are precious to us,
and this separation will involve sorrow and pain.
The blessings and gifts
that are eternally valid, however,
will never be taken from us.
The gift of God's Son,
the eternal hope renewed in His resurrection,
the presence of His Spirit,
the salvation which is already ours—
these gifts are ours forever and ought to fill
our lives with perpetual praise.

It is important, then,
whatever happens to us in our world,
that our hope be focused firmly upon God
and that our lives
be involved in His eternal objectives.
He is truly our Father, and we are at all times
to be His obedient children and servants.
He paid the price of our redemption and adoption.
We belong to Him; we are His possessions.

May our faith,
    tested constantly by the hot fires of adversity,
    be enlarged and increased.
May our love be made more honest and generous.
And may it be our do-or-die determination to please
    God and serve our fellow persons
    regardless of the cost or consequence to our lives.

1 Peter 2

We, who have sampled God's grace and know that He accepts
    us as His children and remembers our sins no more,
    are just beginning to realize the magnitude
    and immensity of that grace.
Now it is time to grow in that grace, to put aside our
    childishness and become mature, dependable Christians.
Like the blocks that firm up and reinforce a building,
    we ought to be the kind of men and women that
    build up God's kingdom on earth.
Our great God has accepted us as His sons and daughters
    and appointed us to be His ministers.
We, with Christ as our Savior and Master,
    are the kingdom of God.

There are, however, many other blocks, still unprepared,
    that need to be shaped and formed and made to fit
    into this great temple of God.
Our Lord has made us the blocks that hold together
    other blocks—and the artisans that assist in hewing
    and shaping others to find their places in this
    structure our God is building.

We are to do this by declaring the love of God for all
people and demonstrating that love in our
sacrificial deeds of kindness on behalf of God
and for the benefit of humanity.

It is this profound responsibility that shapes our lives
and guides our activities in our remaining years
upon this planet.
While God and His will is supreme,
we are to subject ourselves to the secular leaders who
justly and lawfully direct the activities of our
community.
We are to live as the free persons that we are
and yet limit that freedom to those matters
that will benefit our fellow persons.
We are to respect our fellow beings,
honorably fulfill the conditions of our secular
employment, respond to abusive people with patience
and kindness, and even endure suffering at the hands
of others with forgiving love.
After all, we can afford to lose our material goods,
worldly acclaim, even our physical lives—
and yet lose nothing at all because we are the
children and ministers of God and belong to Him forever.
Whereas our peers may regard us as weaklings when we
respond in gentleness and meekness to the abuse that
comes our way, our Lord has by example revealed this
as His way of advancing God's kingdom and has
challenged us to live and to serve as He did before us.
This is the way of love that drew us into the
family of God;
let us walk in it.

1 Peter 3

We who are married ought to begin demonstrating our love
    to our fellow persons in our relationship to our mates.
If we can't make it as husbands and wives,
    our community will not likely take our public
    declarations of Christian love and concern
    very seriously.
A marriage relationship may well prove an excellent
    testing ground and training program
    for all interpersonal relationships.
If we faithfully assume our particular roles and accept
    our mates as equals in every respect,
    and strengthen, support and encourage them in
    our marital relationships,
    we have a strong foundation for effective, life-giving,
    love-sharing relationships to others about us.

Married or not, we are all members of the same family,
    the family of God, and members of Christ's body;
    and we ought to relate and interrelate with one
    another like the parts of our individual physical
    bodies, which harmoniously work together to promote
    our health and well-being.
This would be the most positive declaration of God's love
    and grace to our secular community,
    and this is a basis for a truly effective ministry
    to a distraught, divisive world about us.

There will, no doubt, be some degree of pain involved in
    our witness to a rebellious world.
There will be reaction as well as response.

Even reaction is better than apathy and may ultimately
    resolve in some growth in our own lives
    as well as progress in the advancement of the kingdom.
The point is,
    whereas there is no call for a martyr complex,
    we need never be ashamed of suffering for Jesus' sake.
It is far better to patiently bear the hurt that others
    inflict upon us than to be the cause of their pain,
    or to be guilty of not making any effort to
    alleviate their suffering.
Here again, Jesus is our example;
    He suffered on our behalf.
Do we, as His disciples, expect to avoid all pain
    in our ministry to our fellow persons?
May God grant to us the kind of love and courage
    to enter into suffering, if such is necessary,
    in order to unscramble God's Word and declare in
    witness and deed His love and salvation for
    disoriented people in a disjointed world.

1 Peter 4

We ought not to be surprised when we are afflicted
    by tragic or troublesome events.
What is happening in our world today—
    with us and our loved ones about us—
    has been the lot of all God's creatures
    throughout the ages.
Jesus Christ Himself, God's beloved Son, suffered much
    in the course of His brief life

168

upon this strife-ridden world.
How dare we expect any less?
It is, therefore, not so tragic or unfortunate
    that we suffer.
It is probable that such suffering
    will enrich our lives and enlarge our faith.
But God forbid that we be the cause of another's pain.
May God forgive us should this happen, and help us
    to rectify our foolishness and carelessness
    and subdue or lessen the suffering we have caused.

It is not possible to comprehend the fateful things
    that happen from time to time.
It is not expected that we do,
    only that we trust Him
    who suffered on our behalf
    and who will be with us in our trials and conflicts.

Sufferings, trials, conflicts come to all of us
    at one time or another.
They cannot be avoided or ignored.
They are real—and they hurt.
But in addition to trusting God
    in the midst of conflicts,
    we can cushion their shock or lessen their hurt
    by holding on to one another, by loving, sharing,
    helping to bear one another's burdens and sufferings.
This is what it means to belong to the family of God.
This is one of our purposes in representing
    and communicating Him in our walk upon this world.
Let us be alert to the needs of one another
    and thereby help one another remain faithful to God.

1 Peter 5

It is expected that we, as God's children and ministers,
   participate in Christ's sufferings on behalf
   of humanity as well as in His glory
   which will ultimately be revealed
   to those who embrace Him as their Savior and Lord.
As Jesus became our leader, so we serve in our arenas or
   parishes of activity, whether they be assigned by God or
   are determined by the circumstances that crowd us,
   and we become ministers—sometimes leaders—
   within our fields of service.
We do not have to come across as leaders
   in every situation; but as ministers, servants to
   people around us, we need to be willing to assume our
   responsibility as God's envoys and representatives,
   His communicators of divine grace to those who
   cross our paths.
Our responsibilities are enormous; the risks are many;
   but we do not have to be afraid for our souls even if
   our bodies are exposed to the atrocities of this world
   and the sometimes frightening reactions
   of its inhabitants.
He will care for us; no one can snatch us out of His
   loving embrace.
This is a promise from God.
We need to be on our guard lest we fall prey to some
   adversary that attempts to breach our relationship
   to God, but we need not be afraid because God truly
   cares about us.
There will be suffering; there is a great God who will

give us the grace to endure it—
and the courage and wisdom we need to serve Him
and our fellow persons through it.

2 Peter 1

Do we really believe
that our great God has granted through His Spirit
everything we need to be happy and contributive
as His children and servants?
It's true!
But like money in some savings account
God's precious gifts remain in the bank
and our lives remain dwarfed and niggardly,
largely dependent upon small talents
and starved by large doubts.
Only by cashing in on God's glorious promises
are we able to live effectively
and productively
in our kind of world.

There are other things
we must stir into the divine recipe
for joyous living in a joyless society.
A large measure of faith must be laced generously
with kindness and goodness.
Added to that must be an ever-open mind,
a searching, reaching grasp for truth.
Courage and fortitude,
a dogged determination to keep going,

a persistent, day-by-day surrender
to God and His purposes,
are necessary for Christian maturity.
Then there must be love—and added to love, more love,
for this is the most important ingredient of all.
It is this that makes for authentic Christianity.
Without these qualities
our witness will have little effect
on the suffering, lonely, loveless, oppressed,
and indifferent inhabitants of this planet.

We certainly ought to be aware of these things
that are needed to make our Christian experience
genuine and permanent.
Nevertheless,
we need occasional reminders and challenges,
for, it seems, we are quick to slack off
when life becomes comfortable or the road ahead
appears a little easier to negotiate.
This may well be one of the reasons our loving God
permits suffering to afflict us;
it keeps our heads straight and our hearts focused
on the truly important goal of our lives,
a right relationship with God.

2 Peter 2

We are greatly disturbed by the innumerable prophets
that plague our generation in their attempt to gain
a following and by the scores of misguided people

who seek entry into our houses in the process of
peddling their man-made concoctions.
The thing that really shakes us up is the manner in which
multitudes of our citizens are falling for it and
buying into this nonsense in the hope that they can
find some tangible handles that will enable them to
manipulate an intangible God.
Most of these prophets of darkness are even very tolerant
about the Christ name—
using it to make some of their offerings
a little more palatable to the man on the street.
An alarming number of them insist that they have the true
Gospel and claim that they are preaching Jesus Christ
when, in effect, they are propagating a gospel of
work-righteousness, a system of dos and don'ts,
rules and regulations which, if observed in their
prescribed manner, will bring order and peace to
the lives of fearful people.
It is not a salvation-by-faith but salvation-by-works
gospel that they are passing off for the truth,
and even many of those who have been in our camp
and who should know better
are swallowing this poison as if it were some newly
discovered key to the portals of life everlasting.

It becomes apparent that faith is hard to come by for
most people; they need someone to take them
by the hand and lead them to the portals of glory.
Maybe it is an endeavor to bypass the struggle that faith
involves, the suffering, the conflicts and pains,
that are integral to the life of following Christ;
the thinking, doubting, trusting, and risking necessary
for anyone who is to carry out the purposes of God.

There is a measure of error in most of our proclamations,
and there is confusion and confoundedness, dialog and
disagreement as we struggle to articulate our
insights and to persist in our truth-seeking in respect
to God and Christ and His will for our lives.
But God forbid that we be content with anything less than
what He wants for us, that we take the easy way out
and climb on those popular bandwagons that promise
heaven in six simple steps and that we dare to pass
on this questionable jargon as Gospel-truth
to others in our paths.
The way of salvation has been made possible through faith
in what Christ has done for us and has been made
plain in His Word to us.
If we accept Him as He is revealed in His Word and commit
ourselves to following Him as He has prescribed,
although we may not all be emulating Him in precisely
the same way, we will be glorifying the same Christ and
will discover far more to unite us than to divide.

We know of only one way to God.
It is the way of faith in God as revealed
through His Son, our Lord.
This is the life that we are committed to live and the
Gospel we are commanded to preach.
For us there is none other—nor need be.
Our God has found us, and we have returned to Him.

2 Peter 3

It is not surprising that we long so intensely
   for the final appearance of our Lord,
   for that great day when we shall be delivered
   from our dissipating bodies
   and destruction-bent world
   to be united totally and eternally with Jesus Christ.
We live in and are threatend by a world of men
   who serve themselves and who are guided
   by their own self-centered passions.
They apparently have no use for God.
They act toward one another as if they were controlled
   by some dark and evil force.
They kill and destroy and leave in their wake
   the mangled minds and bodies
   of their hapless victims.
And yet our Lord tarries;
   His purposes upon this world and through us
   in this world are not yet consummated.
We fearfully acknowledge the terrible things
   that are happening around us
   and cry out in desperation for our blessed Lord's
   intervention in mankind's dark and devilish doings.
Still our Lord tarries,
   and we even begin to doubt
   that He will ever come again.

We need not fear or doubt.
He will come—and in His own good time.
It may be tomorrow, maybe a thousand years from now,
   but He will come.

When He does come, it will be suddenly and unexpectedly
    and, for the masses of men
    who live by their own wills and wits,
    it will be a time of final, fearful judgment.

Maybe we should regard our Lord's tarrying,
    His slowness to act, in terms of purging
    the wickedness of our world,
    as evidence of His loving patience.
He is still waiting for people, and this may include many
    of our friends and relatives,
    to separate themselves
    from the degradation of this planet
    and return to His orbit for their lives.
The desire of His loving heart is that they, too,
    will be ready to meet Him when He returns.

We do not know the year or the day or the hour.
We only know that we belong to Him.
As long as we continue
    to live committed and dedicated lives
    and faithfully and joyfully labor
    within His purposes,
    we are ready for His coming and may,
    in thereby obediently serving Him and our fellow person,
    bring closer that great day of His final
    and ultimate revelation.

1 John 1

How do we know that life in Christ is the real thing?
Is it something we've been brainwashed to accept?
Where does God fit in?
How can we possibly swallow this irrational God-stuff
    in a world of computers and satellites,
    and suffering, starving, dying people?
I speak for myself, yet I can say the same
    for many of you;
    we know that Christ is real,
    that God is alive and well and lovingly concerned
    about each of us,
    because we have seen Him through the eyes of faith,
    have witnessed His miracles in our lives
    or the lives of others around us,
    and have experienced His forgiving and life-giving
    love in our own hearts.
We know Him; He is real to us,
    and He is the source of our joy!

It is this grand experience that we are dedicated
    to share with others,
    the experience of loving fellowship with God,
    of reconciliation and restoration of His plan
    and destiny for His children.
It is, as well, an ever-growing and enriching experience
    that confirms our personal worth as God's redeemed
    children and draws us into a warm and loving
    relationship with one another.
Above all, it reveals to us the meaning of forgiveness,
    of God's acceptance of us just as we are.

We no longer fear God's judgment,
     His anger or displeasure over our sins and failures.
Our Savior, Jesus Christ, has borne that on our behalf.
Our greatest concern is that He who through Christ
     accepts us as we are will ever have His way with us
     and makes us into everything He wants us to be.

1 John 2

Our sins and failures do not need to come
     between us and God.
There will be failings from time to time;
     we must recognize and acknowledge them and claim anew
     the forgiveness that comes through Jesus Christ.
Then we must commit ourselves once more,
     and every day of our lives,
     to trust and obedience.
We can always be sure of God's acceptance;
     He will never let us down.

If our commitment is genuine, however,
     it will be to our Lord's pattern and style of living.
Our Lord lived by one basic commandment,
     one system of morality;
     it was the commandment and morality of love.
He who revealed to us His Father's love
     commanded us to love, to live and serve in love.
The follower of Jesus Christ will not consciously
     entertain any thoughts of bigotry or prejudice.
If he does, he will not long be a follower of Christ.

Hatred, apathy, insensitivity, bigotry, indifference,
  when such characterize attitudes and relationships
  to one's fellow persons,
  are the demons of darkness.
And if they are allowed to enter our lives,
  they will most surely cut us off from God or betray our
  professed relationship to Him to be a gigantic lie.

We must not allow our energies and affections to be
  sapped by the ephemeral attractions of this world.
If it happens, it will drain us of spiritual power—
  that divine energy destined for divine purposes
  and expressed in loving relationships
  with our fellow beings.
Jesus Christ is our Savior and Master.
He has poured out His Spirit upon us.
We must not allow anyone, whatever his intentions,
  to confuse us by casting doubt
  upon this splendid truth.
We are God's children,
  the brothers and sisters of Jesus Christ.
If we follow Him and live as He would have us to live,
  nothing can disrupt or destroy that status.

1 John 3

The fact is we are God's children now!
This status and relationship is not something
  we work for or wait for, it is ours here and now.
It is the gift and consequence of God's love.

Because of this fabulous truth,
 we need never question our identity
 or doubt our validity.
We are and shall be members of the family of God forever.

As God's children, then, we can no longer entertain
 those things that are grievous to Him.
Nor can we expend our energies upon, or dedicate our lives to,
 those matters or projects that do not serve Him.
This does not mean that we avoid our world
 or flee from its hazards and risks.
Armored in God's grace
 and supported by the love and concern
 of our comrades,
 we, as God's soldiers and servants,
 enter into our arena of daily conflict
 to bring God's grace and love to bear
 upon the victims
 of this world's atrocities and obscenities.

Because we are God's children and servants,
 citizens of another Kingdom,
 loyal to that divine Kingdom,
 it is not surprising
 that the world regards us as aliens
 and resents our presence and ministry.
We have discovered our identity and significance
 as God's children.
We do not have to be fearful
 of this world's condemnations
 or be dependent upon its acceptance.
Our response to its enmity is self-sacrificing love.
It may mean our eventual crucifixion as it did for
 our Lord and so many of His followers.

It also means we are thereby adopting God's design
   and following His destiny for our lives,
   an exciting, risk-filled style of living
   that guarantees freedom and joy
   in the midst of this world's oppression and pain.
Above all, it means that we cease spewing platitudes
   and begin to demonstrate our love for our fellow person.
When we are wide open to God and His grace
   and to our fellow person and his needs,
   then we know we are seeking, embracing,
   and living the truth in our lives.

It is obviously not enough to make confessions
   and proclamations concerning our Christian faith.
While we are saved by faith—not works—
   a genuine faith in God
   is clearly marked by obedience.
We live in obedience to God when,
   while believing in Him,
   we lovingly and actively reach out to meet the
   needs of our fellow persons.
Apart from this level of obedience,
   one's faith is very much in question
   and so is one's relationship to God.

1 John 4

After all is said and done,
   the proof of our adoption of God's children is love.
This begins with our acceptance of God's love

as it is revealed and granted to us
through Jesus Christ.
It is further revealed and extended through
our love for one another.
This is what the God-life is all about.
Apart from God there is no real love;
apart from love God is not real in us
and is not able to work through us.
If we assume we can continue to bask in God's love
even while we harbor hateful or unloving thoughts
about a brother or sister,
we are deceiving ourselves.

We live in a fear-ridden world and we foolishly allow
these fears to permeate our lives and polarize us
in our interpersonal relationships.
If God's love truly dominates our lives,
this will not happen because it crowds out all fear
and unites us to God and to each other.
God's love is perfect—and He loves perfectly.
This is the manner in which He loves us.
Not only should this free us from the fears
that plague our world, but free us to love
our fellow person without concern for consequences.
This is our assignment in our world today,
to be, as was Christ in His visible visitation,
love incarnate in a love-starved society.
Let us begin by genuinely loving one another.

1 John 5

We who have committed our lives to God as He is revealed
    through Jesus Christ *are* the children of God.
As children of the same Father,
    we are brothers and sisters;
    in loving our divine Parent we also love each other.
When we allow something to come between ourselves and
    each other, that something obscures and may cloud
    our relationship to God.
    We demonstrate our love of God—
    and respond to His love—
    by living in obedience to His commandments.
Because we obey as a response to love, we obey joyfully
    even when our obedience leads us
    to suffering and conflict.
And we are assured that our obedience
    will lead to victory over the rebellious,
    anti-God forces of this world.

We know we are the children of God—
    not by the testimony of men but by the witness
    of God Himself.
He has given His Son, who, through His death and
    resurrection, redeemed us from sin and death and
    by way of the Holy Spirit inhabits our beings.
We claim this and yield to these gifts of God by faith,
    not by sight, our faith in what God has done on our
    behalf, not in what we presume to do for Him.
Thus we know that we *have* eternal life.
It is not some future possibility that we aspire to,
    it is ours at this moment and shall be ours forever.

It is as His sons and daughters that we have perpetual
    access to Him.
He knows our every need; He hears our every prayer.
When we pray within His will and according to His
    purposes, He responds to our requests
    even when such response is made in ways
    our finite spirits cannot comprehend.

Every part of our finite natures that we commit to Him
    is under His loving control.
It is those things we fail to place under His control
    and guidance that cause us trouble from time to time.
Let us be sure that every exposure concerning our
    fallible beings resolves in renewed dedication and
    commitment to our Lord that we might grow in grace
    and become increasingly like the Christ
    who goes before us.
And let us help one another in our walk with God.

2 and 3 John

The children of God are seekers of truth.
Those who are genuinely seeking the truth will
    ultimately become the children of God.
That truth has been revealed through God's Son,
    Jesus Christ.
He shows us the way and He is the way to God.
Whereas our great God has not yet fully revealed Himself,
    He has revealed enough of Himself,
    all that we need and as much as we can possibly

relate to, through Christ.
Only Jesus Christ, God incarnate,
    has been able to put the truth into the form that
    humanity can assimilate and experience.
Any and all of the attempts to discover truth and God
    apart from this Christ are doomed to failure and
    only lead people astray.
Anyone who attempts to entice us into traveling some
    other path in our search for truth must be resisted
    and, unless we are sure of where we stand,
    had better be avoided.

The most effective way of proclaiming the truth that
    we have discovered through Christ is by way of
    loving one another and loving our fellow persons even
    if they are strangers in our midst.
This, in essence, sums up the commandments of our God,
    and in the demonstration of such love we thereby
    fulfill His commandments.
Above all,
    let us love and support our fellow truth-seekers
    and truth-proclaimers,
    our sisters and brothers in Christ.

Jude

We must be aware in these latter days when people are
    confused and frightened by the things that are
    happening, when governments become corrupt
    and institutions fall apart, when the securities

men and women pin their lives and hopes upon are
decimated, that there are false shepherds arising
in every corner of the globe claiming the insight
and ability to lead people back to sanity and order
once more.
Their frenzied minds dream up dreams that rapidly become
religions, and people, like helpless sheep, follow
their foolish doctrines into dark tunnels from which
they may never emerge.
This is happening even within the churches that profess
to honor our Christ.
In adding to or detracting from God's revelation
through His Son, self-appointed prophets attract
the befuddled minds of well-intentioned people
and cheat them out of the joy and freedom,
even the conflicts and sufferings that become the
inheritance of God's true sons and daughters.
There are false prophets amongst us, and we must acquire
from God the discernment to ferret them out and
label them accordingly.

Over against the purveyors of false doctrines and the
disgruntled and malcontent who seek to invade our
fellowship and divide even the faithful,
setting them against one another, are those sincere,
open-minded, humble, loving seekers of truth who have
found and are following the truth as revealed
through Christ.
They are found in some number in most Christian churches
and even outside of the institutional church.
We are of that discipline and must continue to be such.
We have the Spirit of God and must allow His Spirit
to keep us mentally alert and inwardly and outwardly
devoted to God and His purposes.

We are enjoined to abide constantly within the love
of God, to love one another,
and to reach out to the confused seekers about us
with the hope that some of them may be drawn
into our circle of joy and love.

We do, indeed, live within a turbulent world,
but we don't have to be afraid.
We praise our great God, who is able to keep us secure
in Him whatever the turmoil and tempests that beset us.
"To the only God,
our Savior through Jesus Christ our Lord,
be glory, majesty, dominion, and authority,
before all time and now and forever. Amen."